ESSENTIAL FISH & SEAFOOD

FROM THE OCEAN TO THE TABLE

MARKS & SPENCER

Marks and Spencer p.l.c.
PO Box 3339
Chester CH99 9QS

shop online
www.marksandspencer.com

ISBN: 978-1-84805-591-9

Printed in China

Designed by Talking Design
Edited by Susanna Tee and Fiona Biggs
Photography by Clive Streeter
Illustrations by Coral Mula
Food styling by Angela Drake, Teresa Goldfinch and Emma Jane Frost

Exclusive Editions Limited would like to thank Bryce Beukers-Stewart and Peter Richardson for permission to reproduce copyright material on the following pages: 4, 7, 8, 10 (Bryce Beukers-Stewart) 9 and 11 (Peter Richardson).

The Marine Conservation Society (MCS) is the UK charity dedicated to protecting our seas, shores and wildlife.

Please join us – visit our website at www.mcsuk.org
Make a difference – choose sustainable seafood www.fishonline.org
Reg Charity No (England and Wales) 1004005
Reg Charity No (Scotland) SC037480
Company Limited by Guarantee (England & Wales) No: 2550966
Registered Office: Unit 3, Wolf Business Park, Alton Road,
Ross-on-Wye HR9 5NB
Tel: 01989 566017
VAT No. 489 1505 17

NOTES FOR THE READER

This book uses both metric and imperial measurements. Follow the same units of measurement throughout; do not mix metric and imperial. All spoon measurements are level: teaspoons are assumed to be 5 ml, and tablespoons are assumed to be 15 ml. Unless otherwise stated, milk is assumed to be semi-skimmed, eggs and individual vegetables such as potatoes are medium and pepper is freshly ground black pepper. Sufferers from liver disease and those with weakened immune systems should never eat raw fish. Likewise, pregnant women, nursing mothers and young children should avoid eating fish raw, especially larger species such as swordfish and tuna, which tend to have high concentrations of mercury. Recipes using raw or very lightly cooked eggs should be avoided by infants, the elderly, pregnant women, convalescents and anyone suffering from an illness. The times given are an approximate guide only. Preparation times differ according to the techniques used by different people and the cooking times may also vary from those given. Optional ingredients, variations or serving suggestions have not been included in the calculations.

CONTENTS

INTRODUCTION

Essential Fish & Seafood is a guide to preparing, cooking and serving every kind of fish and shellfish. Confirmed fish devotees will be delighted to have some of their favourite, classic recipes in one volume, together with a range of new, and imaginative ideas, while those who may find fish preparation rather daunting will be enlightened, reassured and inspired.

The Fish Directories at the front of chapters one to four introduce the fabulous wealth of healthy, delicious food that our waters – both fresh and sea – can offer. The collection of recipes that follows caters for every meal type and occasion and encompasses popular cuisines from around the globe.

AN INTRODUCTION TO THE MARINE CONSERVATION SOCIETY

Marine Conservation Society

The Marine Conservation Society (MCS) is the UK charity dedicated to the protection of our seas, shores and the wildlife that depends on them. MCS campaigns for clean seas and beaches, sustainable fisheries, protection of marine life and their habitats, and the sensitive use of our marine resources for future generations.

What MCS does

The coastal and marine environments of the UK are some of the most beautiful in the world, supporting an astonishing diversity of habitats and species, as well as providing vital resources for economic development, food and recreation. However, our coastal habitats are under increasing pressure from development, tourism and climate change, while further offshore, marine habitats and species are threatened by activities associated with fisheries, aggregate extraction and offshore energy developments.

Through education and community involvement – from marine-life surveys to beach cleans and litter surveys – and collaboration, MCS helps to raise awareness of the many threats that face our marine environment and promotes various types of action at individual, industry and government level to ensure that our seas are fit for life and will remain so in the future.

Fishing for the future

Healthy fish stocks are a vital part of the marine ecosystem, and provide protein and livelihoods for billions of people. Globally, fisheries supply over 2.6 billion people with at least 20 per cent of their average protein intake.

Overfishing is a significant and growing threat to marine biodiversity and many fish stocks are widely reported to be in a state of serious decline. As well as reducing stocks and ultimately affecting the livelihoods of those working in the industry, the methods used can also have devastating impacts on habitats and non-target species such as dolphins, marine turtles and birds, as a result of dredging and by-catch.

Annually, over 45.5 million metric tonnes – 43% of the seafood destined for dinner tables worldwide – are currently produced by fish farms. Increasing global demand for fish and the limited quantity of wild fish stocks mean that fish-farm production is expected to double by 2030. After Chile and Norway, the UK is the third largest producer of farmed Atlantic salmon.

By raising awareness of the issues surrounding fishing and fish farming and promoting sustainable seafood consumption, MCS aims to encourage more sustainable fisheries management and practices, securing a long-term future for our fisheries and marine environment.

Protection of marine habitats and species

Although the UK's seas support a variety of life as fascinating and colourful as that found anywhere in the world, providing a home for over 8,000 species, we know very little about the marine environment.

Consequently, protection of marine habitats and species has not kept pace with that of our terrestrial landscapes and wildlife, and our activities are wreaking damage on a significant scale. The MCS Biodiversity Programme uses surveys, education and policy development to ensure that marine species and habitats are afforded protection before it's too late. The programme includes:

- the study of rare yet important species
- campaigning for sanctuaries for marine life – marine reserves – where nothing can be done that would damage marine life. The only marine reserve in the UK at present is at Lundy Island
- campaigning for the introduction of new marine laws to protect marine

wildlife and habitats and to ensure the sustainable management of seas and resources

• engaging in vital marine turtle conservation and research and supporting turtle conservation projects around the world.

Pollution-free seas

Toxic chemicals, sewage, crude oil, radioactive waste, agricultural fertilizers, animal waste, storm run-off from our city streets and millions of tonnes of litter all threaten our seas and shoreline. Pollution can contaminate the fish we eat, the water in which we swim and the beaches we visit.

For over 20 years MCS has campaigned in the UK for clean seas and beaches, encouraging everyone to take an active role to prevent further damage.

Community action for clean seas and beaches

Walk along a UK beach and, on average, you'll find 2,000 pieces of litter per kilometre. Beach litter is now a global problem that has a major impact on wildlife, and costs the UK millions of pounds annually in clean-up costs.

MCS has run the Adopt-A-Beach and Beachwatch campaigns since 1993, involving thousands of volunteers in beach cleans and litter surveys every year. It has been able to target specific sources of litter, influence government policy and industry practices, helping to develop solutions to this modern environmental hazard.

The annual MCS *Good Beach Guide* aims to stop the dumping of raw sewage at sea by promoting beaches with the best water quality, recommending beaches that we think

are now clean enough for swimming. There's only one charity in the UK that cares for all of our seas, shores and wildlife – MCS. MCS works for sustainable fisheries, clean seas and beaches, protection of marine life and the sensitive use of our marine

resources so that they will benefit future generations. Everyone, from individuals to businesses, can support MCS – please go to **www.mcsuk.org** or contact MCS (see the imprint page of this book for contact details).

WHY BUY SUSTAINABLE FISH?

Overfishing and stock depletion

The impact of overfishing on fish stocks and the wider marine environment is an issue of growing global concern. A greater demand for fish as world populations increase and people become aware of the health benefits of eating fish, and other influences such as climate change, are also all contributing to overfishing.

For example, Atlantic cod is listed as a threatened and declining species in the Greater North and Celtic Seas. In the North Sea the stock has declined by 75 per cent since the 1970s. Scientists recommend that this fishery must be closed if the stock is to recover. However, only about 30 per cent of the cod landed by UK vessels into the UK and abroad is caught in the North Sea. Most of the rest of

Eco-friendly fish is fish that is caught in such a way as to have no harmful effect on the stock, the marine environment or other species. By choosing only fish from healthy, responsibly managed sources, caught using methods that minimize damage to the marine environment and other species, consumers can help drive the market for sustainably produced seafood and make a real difference to the way our fish stocks are managed.

the cod eaten in Britain is imported from areas such as the Barents and Norwegian Seas, where stocks are more sustainably managed. Landings of haddock, whiting and saithe from the North Sea have all declined since the 1970s and 1980s; indeed, North

Sea mackerel has struggled to recover from the collapse of the fishery in the 1970s and closures remain in place to protect the stock. The common skate, paradoxically, is now becoming very rare in UK shallow seas and in European waters.

The situation in the North Sea, however, has to be balanced with a more positive situation in other UK fisheries, for example in the waters off the southwest coast of England, where there is an increasing understanding of, and a progression towards, more sustainable fisheries.

Impact of fishing on marine species and habitat

Every year hundreds of thousands of marine mammals, turtles and seabirds are killed needlessly in fishing gears all over the world. In many cases these deaths could be avoided, or at least reduced, by introducing the use of 'dolphin-', 'turtle-' and 'seabird-friendly' devices, or by banning the use of damaging practices and by introducing areas in which fishing is prohibited. Similarly, in fisheries where by-catch of seabirds, especially

The fish are fed either by hand or by using automated feed systems. All waste and, in some instances, uneaten feed falls through the bottom of the cages to the seabed below. The cages can be damaged during storms or by accidents, which can lead to fish escaping, causing problems for depleted wild salmon stocks as a result of interbreeding and increased competition for food.

MCS Sustainable Seafood Programme

MCS has raised the profile of several important fisheries issues, including 'no take' zones or the introduction of marine reserves to protect fish stocks and habitat, the unsustainability of deep-water fisheries and, most recently, the consumers' role in making environmentally informed choices about the fish they eat, thus increasing support for sustainable fisheries. As the overfishing crisis deepens, the need for the education of consumers to increase demand for responsibly produced seafood has become ever more important.

Fishonline.org

Following the publication of the *Good Fish Guide* in 2002, MCS launched **www.fishonline.org** in August 2004. The website provides information on over 150 species of fish and shellfish, advice on the status of individual species and/or stocks and a rating based on their relative sustainability. The website also features a list of Fish to Eat and Fish to Avoid, based on the ratings applied through the Fishonline system. A summary of fishonline.org is provided in the handy Pocket Good Fish Guide which can be used when out and about, whether eating at a restaurant, fish and chip shop, or doing the weekly shop.

albatross, is problematic, simple practical measures have been devised to help prevent seabirds being hooked and drowned on longlines.

The most widely used and energy-intensive of all fishing methods is trawling. Examples of fishing methods that directly affect the seabed are bottom trawling, beam trawling and dredging. Depending on the nature of the seabed in which these gears are used, the damage to fragile habitats such as cold-water corals and seamounts can be substantial and irreversible. By restricting their use to areas where the seabed is less sensitive and by adopting measures to reduce the negative impacts associated with them, these fishing methods can be made more sustainable.

Socio-economic consequences

About 60 per cent of the global catch comes from the waters of developing countries where marine resources are often the only wealth. As the overfishing crisis in waters of developed countries deepens and demand for fish intensifies, there is increasing pressure on the fishery resources of developing countries. In Europe, for example, a significant proportion of the fish consumed is imported from developing countries. Meanwhile, in the UK, as a result of the industrialization of fisheries and overfishing, the number of fishermen has reduced by 47 per cent in recent years, from 23,990 in 1981 to 12,647 in 2005, leaving once vibrant and bustling harbours lying idle.

Fish farming

Fish farming is often suggested as the solution to the rising demand for fish. Done well it is part of the solution, done badly it is part of the problem. In the UK, marine fish such as salmon and cod are transferred as juveniles from hatcheries to sea pens or cages where they are grown on to harvest size. The pens are suspended in the sea in inshore waters and have a constant flow of water through them.

INCREASING THE SUSTAINABILITY OF THE FISH YOU EAT

Consumers can make a real difference to the way our fish stocks are managed. When deciding which fish to eat, consider what it is, where it was caught and how.

Biology and life history

Avoid eating species that are long-lived, slow-growing, late to mature and therefore vulnerable to overfishing. Examples of these types of fish include orange roughy, sharks, skates and some species of ray.

Seasonality

Avoid eating fish during their breeding season. Details of when fish breed are available at the MCS website **www.fishonline.org.**

Size and maturity

Size matters! Avoid eating immature, small, undersized fish and shellfish that have not yet had the chance to reproduce or breed. For more information on the size at which many fish species mature, go to **www.fishonline.org.**

Stock status

Avoid eating fish from depleted stocks. When buying fish you need to be aware that, while certain species are overfished in one area, the situation may not be as bad in another, for example haddock (overfished in the West of Scotland and Faroe Islands but sustainable from the Northeast Arctic).

Fishing method

Where possible, choose the most selective or sustainable fishing method available. When choosing haddock for example, which is generally fished together with cod, whiting and saithe, choose line-caught fish as this reduces the number of cod taken as by-catch. This is especially important where the cod stock is depleted.

Know what you are eating

Often fish is labelled with the generic or family name for the species, for example tuna. There are seven commercially available species of tuna, three of which are listed by IUCN (World Conservation Union). Bigeye has been assessed as vulnerable; Northern Bluefin as endangered in the East Atlantic and critically endangered in the

V-notching is the removal of a small piece of tail segment from the tail of an egg-bearing or 'berried' lobster which, if caught, is returned to the sea to continue breeding.

Organic

The organic label applies only to farmed seafood, as only the production of farmed fish can be controlled. The main certification body in the UK, the Soil Association, currently certifies a range of species, including salmon and trout, while standards for other species are under development. Other organic seafood products available in the UK, such as warm water prawns, are certified by other European bodies such as Natureland in Germany.

Organic farming practices meet high environmental standards, including strict limits and restrictions on the use of medicines, chemicals and sea-lice treatments. Feed is sourced sustainably and the number of fish in the cages is generally fewer than on non-organic farms.

Freedom Food certification

The RSPCA scheme to ensure high welfare standards are implemented and maintained for farmed animals.

A set of standards has been developed for farmed salmon that is based around the Farm Animal Welfare Council's five principles:
• freedom to express normal behaviour
• freedom from fear and distress
• freedom from hunger and malnutrition
• freedom from discomfort and pain
• freedom from injury and disease.

West Atlantic and is also listed by OSPAR as a threatened and declining species; and Southern Bluefin is assessed as critically endangered (see the Good Fish Guide on page 12–13). Also yellowfin tuna is listed as 'least concern' and albacore is listed as 'vulnerable' in the North Atlantic and 'critically endangered' in the South Atlantic.

Look at the label

Look for seafood products bearing the Marine Stewardship Council (MSC) label – The Fish with the Blue Tick. The role of the MSC is to recognize well managed fisheries, via a certification programme, and to harness consumer purchasing power to promote environmentally responsible fisheries. See **www.msc.org** for information.

Farmed fish

When eating farmed fish such as trout, carp and warm water prawns, look out for the organic label. Scottish rope-grown mussels are a good choice as the methods used in their production have little environmental impact.

US-farmed catfish are also a good choice in terms of sustainability, as they are farmed in closed inland ponds using re-circulating freshwater, both of which processes prevent escapes and disease transfer. Catfish are also fed a primarily vegetarian diet, which reduces pressure on wild fish caught for fish-feed production.

Lobsters, while not farmed, can be ranched or enhanced. In Cornwall, the National Lobster Hatchery at Padstow releases 5–10,000 juvenile lobsters each year to boost wild stocks and to maintain a sustainable fishery for this species. Tagging or V-notching schemes have also been adopted on a regional basis to protect egg-bearing female lobsters.

GOOD FISH GUIDE
www.fishonline.org

Fish to eat...
Fish from well-managed, sustainable stocks. Dark green indicates species that are, in MCS' opinion, the best choice and lighter green the next best choices.

Fish to eat with caution...
Fish from fisheries that are at risk of becoming unsustainable due to environmental, management or stock issues. MCS recommends that you only eat these fish occasionally. The lighter yellow represents the better choice.

Fish to avoid...
Fish from unsustainable, overfished, vulnerable and/or badly managed fisheries, and/or with high levels of by-catch. In MCS' opinion it is best to avoid these fish at present.

KEY Marine Stewardship Council certified   Dolphin friendly   Soil Association Certified

SPECIES	EAT	CAUTION	AVOID
Abalone	Farmed	-	-
Alaska or walleye pollock	MSC certified	-	-
Anchovy	-	Portuguese coast	Bay of Biscay
Bib or pouting	●	-	-
Black bream, porgy or seabream	●	-	-
Clam	American hardshell and manila, hand-gathered farmed sources	Dredge caught	-
Cockle	MSC certified or hand gathered	Dredge caught	-
Cod, Atlantic	-	Wild caught from N.E. Arctic Wild caught from Iceland, W. English Channel, Bristol Channel, S.E. Ireland & Sole	Wild caught from all other areas

SPECIES	EAT	CAUTION	AVOID
Cod, Pacific	MSC certified	-	-
Coley or saithe	MSC certified	From Iceland or Faroes	-
Crab	Edible/brown, pot caught from S. Devon Spider, pot caught	Edible/brown, pot caught	-
Dab	●	-	-
Dublin Bay prawn, scampi or langoustine	MSC certified	W. Scotland, N. Sea, Skaggerak & Kattegat	From Spain & Portugal
Flounder	●	-	-
Gurnard	Grey & red	Yellow or tub	-
Haddock	-	N.E. Arctic & N. Sea, Skaggerak & Kattegat	From Faroes and W. Scotland
Hake	-	Cape, MSC certified European, northern stock	European, southern stock
Halibut	-	Pacific, MSC certified	Atlantic, wild caught
Halibut, Greenland	-	From N.E. Arctic	From N.W. Atlantic & Greenland, Iceland, W. Scotland & Azores
Herring or Sild	From Norwegian stocks	MSC certified	South Clyde, W. Ireland, & Great Sole fisheries
Ling	-	Handline caught from Faroes	All other stocks
Lobster	Western Australian rock, MSC certified	European, pot caught European, net caught	From Canadian & S. New England stocks

SPECIES	EAT	CAUTION	AVOID
Mackerel	-	MSC cert.	-
Monkfish or anglerfish	-	From S.W. UK & N.E. USA	N./N.W. Spain & Portugal
Mussel, Common	Rope grown or hand gathered	-	-
Oyster	Farmed native & Pacific	-	-
Pollack or lythe		-	-
Plaice	-	Otter trawled from Irish Sea, or gill/seine net from N. Sea	W. English Channel, Celtic Sea, S.W. Ireland & W. Ireland
Prawn	Coldwater, from N.E. Arctic	Tiger, organically farmed / Coldwater, from N. Pacific	Tiger, farmed & wild caught
Ray	-	Cuckoo and spotted from North Sea, Skaggerak, E. English Channel & Celtic Sea; Starry from North Sea, Skaggerak, & E. English Channel	Smalleyed & thornback from Bay of Biscay; all blonde, sandy, shagreen & undulate
Red mullet	From N.E. Atlantic	From Mediterranean	-
Salmon	Pacific (5 species are MSC certified) / Organically farmed	Atlantic, farmed	Atlantic, wild caught
Sardine or pilchard	From Cornwall	From Spain & Portugal	-
Sea bass	Line caught	Farmed	Pelagic trawled
Seabream	-	Organically farmed	Red or blackspot

SPECIES	EAT	CAUTION	AVOID
Skate	-	-	
Snapper	Red (from W. Australia trap fishery) / Malabar blood from W. Australia	Vermillion and lane / Silk and yellowtail	Cubera, mutton and Northern red
Sole	Common or Dover, MSC certified / Lemon, otter trawl caught	Common or Dover, from E. English Channel and S.W. Ireland	Common or Dover from North Sea & Irish Sea
Squid	Jig caught	Trawl caught	-
Swordfish	-	-	Indian Ocean, Mediterranean, and Central & W. Pacific
Tilapia	Farmed	-	-
Trout	Brown or sea and rainbow, organically farmed	Brown or sea and rainbow, farmed	Brown or sea, wild caught from Baltic
Tuna, albacore	MSC certified	From N. Pacific / Pole & Line from N. Atlantic	Longline & pelagic trawled from Mediterranean, N. & S. Atlantic
Tuna, bigeye	-	Handline and pole & line from Central and W. Pacific	All other stocks
Tuna, bluefin	-	-	
Tuna, skipjack	Pole & line from W./Central Pacific or Maldives	From Indian Ocean	Purse seine from W. Atlantic
Tuna, yellowfin	-	Purse seine from Indian Ocean or E. Pacific / All other stocks	-
Turbot	-	Farmed	Wild caught

BUYING AND STORING FISH

Buying

Freshness is the all-important factor to consider when buying any seafood that hasn't been preserved for long-term storage. Fresh fish is highly perishable so, unless you have access to supplies as they are landed, much of the 'fresh' fish for sale will have been frozen on the fishing vessel and then thawed. It is vitally important for you to know the signs of fish in prime condition and those specimens that you should avoid.

Whether you are buying your seafood at a supermarket's fish counter, from a fishmonger or from a market stall, the display slab should be spotlessly clean and there should be plenty of crushed ice around the seafood. Whole, gutted fish deteriorate less quickly than steaks or fillets, so look for a display that includes these.

Your nose will give you the first indication of what you should or shouldn't buy. Good-quality fish has a fresh, ocean-like aroma. It shouldn't smell 'fishy'. If there is any whiff of ammonia or unpleasantness, don't buy. The odour is caused by bacteria rapidly multiplying as the fish deteriorates.

Whole fish should be firm, not floppy, and the flesh should feel firm and elastic when you press gently. The eyes should be protruding and clear, not sunken or cloudy; any scales should be shiny and tight against the skin; the gills should be clear and bright red, not dull or grey. Fillets and steaks should be cleanly cut and look moist and fresh, with a shiny 'bloom' on the surface and no yellowing or browning.

Never buy packaged fish with damaged packaging. There should not be much air between the fish and the wrapping or any pools of liquid or blood. And, of course, you should check the use-by date.

The term 'shellfish' includes a wide range of specimens – bivalves (clams, mussels, oysters, scallops), crustaceans (crabs, lobsters, prawns) and cephalopods (squid and octopus) – they should all be consumed on the day of purchase.

When clams, mussels and oysters are sold alive, the shells should be tightly closed; if open shells don't snap shut when tapped, they are dead. They should be in a net or porous bag, not a polythene bag. Most scallops are sold shucked, often with the roe attached, but

occasionally in the shell. Shrimp and Dublin Bay prawns are often sold frozen, but can also be raw or cooked. It is best to buy them in the shell – look for firm flesh, and avoid any with black spots on the shells (except in the case of large black tiger prawns). Squid and octopus are both sold fresh and frozen – the flesh shouldn't have any brown patches. Both smell foul if not fresh.

Make sure the packaging on sealed, smoked seafood isn't damaged and that the use-by date hasn't expired. If buying loose, it shouldn't have an unpleasant smell or dry edges. If salt cod is still flexible when you buy, wrap it in a damp towel and chill for up to three weeks; if it is rigid, wrap in foil and chill for up to three months. Always check the best-before dates on canned seafood.

Safe storage

Get your purchase home and refrigerated as soon as possible, ideally transporting it in an insulated bag. Remove all packaging and clean the fish with a damp cloth, then wrap it in wet kitchen paper and place on a lipped plate at the bottom of the fridge, at a temperature no higher than 4°C/40°F.

Leave live clams, mussels and oysters in their bag or put them in a dry bowl and cover with wet kitchen paper. Do not put them in a bowl of water or a sealed container, as they will die. Store oysters in their shells, rounded cup down, to keep them fresh in their juices, covered with a wet cloth or seaweed.

All shellfish should be stored in the bottom of the fridge and cooked or eaten within 12 hours. Fresh fish should also be cooked and eaten on the day of purchase, although most remain edible for another day if properly refrigerated. Oily fish spoils more quickly than white fish.

Refrigerate smoked or marinated seafood as soon as you get it home, and consume within two or three days, or by the use-by date.

WAYS TO COOK FISH

The Canadian Cooking Theory, developed some decades ago, advocates cooking fish for 10 minutes per 2.5 cm/1 inch at the thickest part for dry-heat methods. This is an easy approach for anyone new to seafood cooking, but many chefs today prefer 8–9 minutes for slightly less well-cooked fish. This is a matter of personal taste, so experiment and know how to tell when fish is cooked as you enjoy it: perfectly cooked fish is opaque with milky white juices and flakes and comes away from the bone easily; undercooked fish resists flaking, is translucent and has clear juices; overcooked fish looks dry and falls apart into thin pieces. Tuna and other meaty fish can be roasted and pan-seared like beef to be served rare, medium and well-done.

When you are chargrilling, sautéing and pan- and stir-frying, start with a well-heated pan or wok, so that the fish develops a crust that retains internal moisture.

Dry-heat cooking – barbecuing, grilling, chargrilling and roasting

Whole fish, fillets, steaks and kebabs can be cooked by these methods, and oily fish are particularly suited to grilling, barbecuing and chargrilling, because the natural oils they contain baste the flesh. Their full flavours are not overpowered by smoky aromas. Marinate white fish before barbecuing.

Barbecuing and grilling are similar, with the former cooking from the bottom and the latter from the top. In both cases, position the rack about 10 cm/4 inches from the heat. Brush the

Unlike meat, fish have naturally tender flesh, so they need very little preparation and cooking. Fish can be cooked in several different ways, but the one thing to guard against is overcooking.

rack with oil, add the fish and cook until the flesh flakes easily, basting with a marinade or melted butter. Ideally cook the fish without turning; if the surface is browning too quickly, adjust the rack position. Barbecue thin fillets and small fish, such as sardines, in a hinged fish basket.

Chargrilling is a quick way to give fish a barbecue flavour without having to light a barbecue. Heat a cast-iron griddle pan over a high heat, brush the fish with oil and chargrill until seared on one side and cooked through.

Whole fish are particularly delicious when roasted, as the skin and bones preserve the natural flavours. Preheat the oven to 230°C/450°F/Gas Mark 8 and make a few slashes on each side. Rub the fish with oil, put in a roasting pan and roast, uncovered, until the flesh comes away from the bone when tested – the skin becomes crisp, while the flesh remains tenderly moist.

Wet-heat cooking – poaching, steaming and stewing

Fish is excellent poached or steamed. Although these techniques are very easy, they can still overcook fish so pay close attention. Another advantage is that the cooking liquid can be incorporated into a tasty sauce to serve alongside. Poach in gently simmering liquid flavoured with

CHARGRILLING

ROASTING

lemon and herbs for 8–12 minutes per 2.5 cm/1 inch of thickness. When steaming, make sure the seasoned fish never actually touches the water. Steam, covered, for 3–5 minutes for fillets and steaks and 8–9 minutes per 2.5 cm/1 inch of thickness for whole fish.

Seafish stews often contain a variety of fish, simmered with other ingredients. To prevent overcooking, add the seafood towards the end, adding the most delicate pieces last – they will take only 2 or 3 minutes. Don't allow the liquid to boil.

Cooking in oil – sautéing, stir-frying and pan- and deep-frying

Fish steaks and fillets are most suited to these quick techniques. For sautéing and pan-frying, heat 5 mm/$\frac{1}{4}$ inch vegetable oil in a hot sauté or frying pan, dust the fish with seasoned flour and fry over medium-high heat for 2–3 minutes on each side for thin fillets, and up to 5–6 minutes per side for steaks 2.5 cm/ 1 inch thick.

Successful deep-frying requires fish to be coated in batter or crumbs and for the oil to be maintained at a steady 180°C/350°F. If you don't have a deep-fat fryer with a controlled thermostat, use a heavy-based pan and a thermometer: if the temperature is too cool, the fried fish will be soggy; if it is too high, the outside will be overcooked while the centre will be raw. Work in batches to prevent overcrowding and a reduction in the oil's temperature.

DON'T FIDDLE WHEN SEARING, CHARGRILLING, GRILLING AND BARBECUING, AND DON'T BE TEMPTED TO TURN OR MOVE THE FISH AROUND WHILE COOKING, AS IT MAY STICK TO THE PAN OR RACK AND FALL APART. IDEALLY, TURN THE FISH ONLY ONCE DURING COOKING.

POACHING

BARBECUING

PAN-FRYING

BASIC RECIPES

The recipes in this book provide a delightful variety of delicious fish meals. Some of the recipes use common basic recipes which are referred to on these pages, or you could use these basic recipes as an addition to a dish of your choice.

FISH STOCK

MAKES ABOUT 1.4 LITRES/2½ PINTS

- 900 G–1.3 KG/2–3 LB FISH HEADS, BONES AND TAILS, WITH ANY LARGE BONES CRACKED AND WITHOUT ANY GILLS
- 1.2 LITRES/2 PINTS WATER
- 500 ML/18 FL OZ DRY WHITE WINE
- 1 ONION, THINLY SLICED
- 1 LEEK, HALVED, RINSED AND CHOPPED
- 1 CARROT, PEELED AND SLICED
- 6 FRESH FLAT-LEAF PARSLEY SPRIGS
- 1 BAY LEAF
- 4 BLACK PEPPERCORNS, LIGHTLY CRUSHED

Put the fish trimmings, water and wine in a large, heavy-based saucepan over a medium–high heat and slowly bring to the boil, skimming the surface constantly to remove the grey foam.

When the foam stops forming, reduce the heat to low, add the remaining ingredients and leave the stock to simmer for 30 minutes, skimming the surface occasionally if necessary. Strain the stock and discard the flavouring ingredients. The stock is now ready to use or can be left to cool completely, then chilled for 1 day, as long as it is brought to a full rolling boil before use. Alternatively, it can be frozen for up to 6 months.

COURT BOUILLON

MAKES ABOUT 0.6 LITRES/1 PINT

- 850 ML/1½ PINTS COLD WATER
- 850 ML/1½ PINTS DRY WHITE WINE
- 3 TBSP WHITE WINE VINEGAR
- 2 LARGE CARROTS, ROUGHLY CHOPPED
- 1 ONION, ROUGHLY CHOPPED
- 2 CELERY STICKS, ROUGHLY CHOPPED
- 2 LEEKS, ROUGHLY CHOPPED
- 2 GARLIC CLOVES, ROUGHLY CHOPPED
- 2 FRESH BAY LEAVES
- 4 FRESH PARSLEY SPRIGS
- 6 BLACK PEPPERCORNS
- 1 TSP SEA SALT

Put all the ingredients into a large saucepan and slowly bring to the boil. Cover and simmer gently for 30 minutes. Strain the liquid through a fine sieve into a clean saucepan. Bring to the boil again and simmer fast, uncovered, for 15–20 minutes, until reduced to 600 ml/1 pint.

Simmer the fish in the court bouillon, according to the length of time required to cook. Drain the fish.

BÉCHAMEL SAUCE

- 300 ML/10 FL OZ MILK
- 4 CLOVES
- 1 BAY LEAF
- PINCH OF FRESHLY GRATED NUTMEG
- 25 G/1 OZ BUTTER OR MARGARINE
- 2 TBSP PLAIN FLOUR
- SALT AND PEPPER

Put the milk in a saucepan and add the cloves, bay leaf and nutmeg. Gradually bring to the boil. Remove from the heat and set aside for 15 minutes.
Melt the butter in another saucepan and stir in the flour to make a roux. Cook gently, stirring, for 1 minute. Remove the pan from the heat.
Strain the milk and gradually blend into the roux. Return the pan to the heat and gently bring to the boil, stirring, until the sauce thickens. Season to taste.

VARIATIONS
All sorts of ingredients can be added to the basic Béchamel recipe to make interesting sauces that go particularly well with vegetables and fish.

WATERCRESS SAUCE
Add a small bunch of watercress, finely chopped, to the basic sauce.

PARSLEY SAUCE
Add 2 tablespoons of finely chopped fresh parsley to the basic sauce.

MUSHROOM SAUCE
Add 115 g/4 oz finely sliced button mushrooms to the basic sauce with 1 tablespoon of finely chopped fresh tarragon.

LEMON SAUCE
Add some finely grated lemon rind and 1 teaspoon of lemon juice to the basic sauce.

MUSTARD SAUCE
Add 1 tablespoon of French mustard and a squeeze of lemon juice to the basic sauce.

HOLLANDAISE SAUCE

- 2 TBSP WHITE WINE VINEGAR
- 2 TBSP WATER
- 6 BLACK PEPPERCORNS
- 3 EGG YOLKS
- 250 G/9 OZ UNSALTED BUTTER
- 2 TSP LEMON JUICE
- SALT AND PEPPER

Put the wine vinegar and water into a small saucepan with the peppercorns, bring to the boil, then reduce the heat and simmer until it is reduced to 1 tablespoon (take care, as this happens very quickly). Strain.
Mix the egg yolks in a blender or food processor and add the strained vinegar while the machine is running.
Melt the butter in a small saucepan and heat until it is almost brown. While the blender is running, add three-quarters of the butter and the lemon juice, then add the remaining butter and season well with salt and pepper.
Turn the sauce into a serving bowl or keep warm for up to 1 hour in a bowl over a saucepan of warm water. If serving cold, allow to cool and store in the refrigerator for up to 2 days.

MAYONNAISE

- 2 EGG YOLKS
- 150 ML/5 FL OZ SUNFLOWER OIL
- 150 ML/5 FL OZ OLIVE OIL
- 1 TBSP WHITE WINE VINEGAR
- 2 TSP DIJON MUSTARD
- SALT AND PEPPER

Beat the egg yolks with a pinch of salt. Combine the oils in a jug. Gradually add one quarter of the oil mixture to the beaten egg, a drop at a time, beating constantly with a whisk or electric mixer.

Beat in the vinegar, then continue adding the combined oils in a steady stream, beating constantly.

Stir in the mustard and season to taste with salt and pepper.

AÏOLI

- 1 LARGE EGG YOLK
- 1 TBSP WHITE WINE VINEGAR OR LEMON JUICE
- 2 LARGE GARLIC CLOVES, PEELED AND CRUSHED
- 5 TBSP EXTRA VIRGIN OLIVE OIL
- 5 TBSP SUNFLOWER OIL
- SALT AND PEPPER

Put the egg yolk, vinegar, garlic, and salt and pepper to taste in a bowl and whisk until all the ingredients are well blended.

Add the olive oil, then the sunflower oil, drop by drop at first, and then, when the sauce begins to thicken, in a slow, steady stream until it is thick and smooth.

GREEK GARLIC SAUCE

- 115 G/4 OZ WHOLE BLANCHED ALMONDS
- 3 TBSP FRESH WHITE BREADCRUMBS
- 2 LARGE GARLIC CLOVES, CRUSHED
- 2 TSP LEMON JUICE
- 150 ML/5 FL OZ EXTRA VIRGIN OLIVE OIL
- 4 TBSP HOT WATER
- SALT AND PEPPER

Put the almonds in a food processor and blend until finely ground. Add the breadcrumbs, garlic, lemon juice, and salt and pepper to taste, and mix well together.

With the machine running, very slowly pour in the oil to form a smooth, thick mixture. When all the oil has been added, blend in the water.

Turn the mixture into a bowl and chill in the refrigerator for at least 2 hours before serving.

TARTARE SAUCE

- 2 LARGE EGG YOLKS
- 2 TSP DIJON MUSTARD
- 2 TBSP LEMON JUICE OR WHITE WINE VINEGAR
- ABOUT 300 ML/10 FL OZ SUNFLOWER OIL
- 10 CORNICHONS, FINELY CHOPPED
- 1 TBSP CAPERS, FINELY CHOPPED
- 1 TBSP FLAT-LEAF PARSLEY, FINELY CHOPPED
- SALT
- WHITE PEPPER

Whiz the egg yolks with the Dijon mustard, and salt and pepper to taste, in a food processor or blender or by hand. Add the lemon juice and whiz again.

With the motor still running or still beating, add the oil, drop by drop at first. When the sauce begins to thicken, the oil can then be added in a slow, steady stream.

Stir in the cornichons, capers and parsley. Taste and adjust the seasoning with extra salt, pepper and lemon juice if necessary. If the sauce seems too thick, slowly add 1 tablespoon of hot water.

Use at once or store in an airtight container in the refrigerator for up to 1 week.

SUSHI RICE

MAKES 1 QUANTITY
- 250 G/9 OZ SUSHI RICE
- 325 ML/11 FL OZ WATER
- 1 PIECE OF KOMBU
- 2 TBSP SUSHI RICE SEASONING

Wash the sushi rice under cold running water until the water running through it is clear, then drain the rice. Put the rice in a saucepan with the water and the kombu, then cover and bring to the boil as quickly as you can. Remove the kombu, then reduce the heat and simmer for 10 minutes. Turn off the heat and leave the rice to stand for 15 minutes. Do not take the lid off the saucepan once you have removed the kombu.

Put the hot rice in a large, very shallow bowl and pour the sushi rice seasoning evenly over the surface of the rice. Use one hand to mix the seasoning carefully into the rice with quick cutting strokes using a spatula, and the other to fan the sushi rice in order to cool it quickly.

The sushi rice should look shiny and be at room temperature when you are ready to use it.

BEURRE BLANC

- 3 TBSP VERY FINELY CHOPPED SHALLOTS
- 2 BAY LEAVES
- 6 BLACK PEPPERCORNS, LIGHTLY CRUSHED
- 3 TBSP WHITE WINE, SUCH AS MUSCADET
- 3 TBSP WHITE WINE VINEGAR
- 1½ TBSP DOUBLE CREAM
- 175 G/6 OZ UNSALTED BUTTER, CUT INTO SMALL PIECES
- 2 TSP CHOPPED FRESH TARRAGON
- SALT AND PEPPER

Put the shallots, bay leaves, peppercorns, wine and vinegar in a small saucepan over a medium–high heat and boil until reduced to about 1 tablespoon. Strain the mixture through a non-metallic sieve, then return the liquid to the saucepan. Stir the cream into the liquid and bring to the boil, then reduce the heat to low. Whisk in the butter, piece by piece, not adding the next until the previous one has melted. Whisking constantly and lifting the pan off the heat occasionally will help to prevent the sauce separating. Stir in the tarragon, and salt and pepper to taste, and serve immediately.

Salmon supreme

It's important to include fish in your diet, but there are worries about harming the marine environment. Keep your conscience clear by choosing Lochmuir™ salmon.

One portion of Lochmuir™ middle cut salmon fillet provides the recommended allowance of Omega-3 fatty acids for the week.

PHOTOGRAPHY SIMON WALTON

Salmon is one of the nation's most popular foods – and it's no wonder. Succulent and full of delicate flavour, it responds well to most cooking methods – baking, steaming, pan-frying and grilling – and is also well [sui]ted to raw fish dishes, such as carpaccio and sushi. Best of all, [sal]mon is highly nutritious. It's a source of protein, B vitamins and [om]ega-3 fatty acids – a form of polyunsaturated fat that may help [m]aintain a healthy heart as part of a healthy lifestyle.

But could our demand for salmon be threatening its future? [Th]ankfully, M&S customers can be confident in what they are [bu]ying. From May 2008, all farmed salmon in M&S products – [fro]m prepared meals to sandwiches, salads and, of course, fresh [sa]lmon – is the Lochmuir™ variety from Scottish Sea Farms. It has [be]en reared with the utmost respect for both the fish and the [en]vironment, and is exclusive to M&S. The result? A truly superior, [he]althy and tasty salmon, with a fresh clean flavour, rich buttery [fl]ish and delicate flaky texture – the perfect ingredient for our [de]licious recipe below.

All farmed M&S salmon is now Lochmuir™ – reared in the clear waters of the western coast of Scotland, the Shetland and Orkney Islands.

Salmon fillets with couscous crust

Preparation 15 minutes
Cooking 10 minutes

4 Lochmuir™ Salmon Fillets
100ml dry white wine
75g couscous
30g pine nuts
10g dill and flat-leaf parsley, [fi]nely chopped

1 Heat the oven to 200°C/[4]00°F/Gas Mark 6 (180°C for [f]an ovens). Put the salmon on [a] buttered baking tray, [e]venly spaced apart.

2 Heat the wine to simmering [p]oint and pour over the [c]ouscous. Leave for [5] minutes, until the liquid [i]s absorbed. Fluff up with [a] fork and stir through the [p]ine nuts and herbs.

3 Evenly cover the tops of [t]he salmon with the mixture [a]nd bake for 10 minutes, [o]r until the salmon is cooked [t]hrough and the couscous [i]s turning golden.

M&S'S TEAM OF BUYERS WORK CLOSELY WITH SCOTTISH SEA FARMS TO HELP PRODUCE SUPERIOR LOCHMUIR™ SALMON

Where does Lochmuir™ salmon come from? Dedicated sites on the west coast of Scotland, and the Shetland and Orkney Islands, where the wild currents of the North Atlantic Ocean create ideal conditions for producing first-class salmon all year round. Eggs are hatched and reared in freshwater hatcheries for six to eight months, before moving into lochs for the remainder of the freshwater cycle (12–15 months). They then move into sea water, where they develop for a further 18–22 months, up to approximately 5kg.

What else makes Lochmuir™ salmon special? **Quality and welfare** M&S farmers work to high standards of fish husbandry to produce affordable, quality salmon. The number of fish in each pen is well below average for the fish-farming industry. **Unique diet** The salmon grow slowly, over three years, and are fed a diet of only natural ingredients. **Freedom Food accreditation** RSPCA's farm assurance scheme recently gave full accreditation to Lochmuir™ salmon – the first producer to achieve this. **Traceability** The care and attention given throughout the fishes' life cycle makes them traceable from egg to pack. **Environmental policy** Farmers work with the Marine Conservation Society to reduce and eliminate negative impacts on wild fish stocks and the environment.

FLAT SEAFISH

Often regarded as the 'king of the seas', because of their fine texture and delicately-flavoured flesh, the fish in this chapter are very low in fat and high in protein. The thin fillets respond well to quick cooking techniques, such as pan-frying, which makes them perfect for quick meals. Another advantage of flat fish is that they are interchangeable in most recipes so if, for example, sole is too expensive, try plaice or halibut.

THE FLAT SEAFISH DIRECTORY

The following is a guide to all the main species of flat fish that can be eaten, listed by their common names, although some fish, confusingly, are known by a variety of different names. The potted profile for each fish details the various forms in which it can be purchased, for example whole or in fillets, fresh or canned, and the most suitable cooking methods.

PLAICE

One of the most popular flat fish, it is distinguished by the large red or orange spots on its brown back. It is available whole or in fillets and its white flesh can be fried, grilled, poached, steamed or baked.

FLOUNDER

Flounder is very similar to plaice, but its flavour and texture are not so fine. It is available whole or in fillets and can be cooked in the same way as plaice. In the US, flounder is a collective name for several varieties of flat fish.

TURBOT

This fish, with its huge brown, knobbly body and small head, is considered the finest of the flat fish. It is low in fat, has firm, snow-white flesh and a fine, delicate taste. Depending on its size, it is available whole, in cutlets or in fillets and can be baked, poached or steamed.

BRILL

Brill is smaller but not dissimilar to turbot in flavour and texture. It is usually sold whole, but can be halved, sliced or filleted and lends itself to being cooked by any method.

SKATE & RAY

This strange-looking fish is shaped like a kite. There are several varieties, of which only the fish's pectoral fins, known as its wings, and small pieces of flesh cut from the bony part of the fish, known as nobs, are eaten. It is low in fat and has a superior flavour. The common skate is particularly vulnerable to overfishing and is listed as endangered (see the best choices to make in the Marine Conservation Society Good Fish Guide on page 12–13).

DOVER SOLE

This is one of the finest-flavoured and finest-textured small flat fish. Its white flesh has an exquisite flavour. Available whole or in fillets, it is traditionally grilled or fried, a classic recipe being Sole Meunière.

HALIBUT

This large flat fish is available whole or as cutlets or fillets. Its flesh is quite oily and its firm texture makes it suitable for a variety of cooking methods, including baking, braising, poaching or steaming. Halibut is vulnerable to overfishing (see the best choices to make in the Marine Conservation Society Good Fish Guide on page 12–13).

DOLPHIN FISH/ MAHI-MAHI/ DORADO

Found in warm waters, this is a stunningly attractive fish with a streamlined silver body and black and gold spots, which fade once it is caught. Small fish are sold whole, whereas larger fish are sold in cutlets and fillets. Its flesh is firm and well flavoured, and it is very versatile as it can be fried, grilled and cooked in a pie.

LEMON SOLE

Lemon sole is not dissimilar to Dover sole, although it has far less flavour, and while its white flesh has a fine texture it is less firm. It can be purchased and cooked in the same way as Dover sole.

DAB

This is one of the smallest flat fish and belongs to the plaice family. It has a rough, light brown upper skin and white flesh. It is available whole or in fillets and can be cooked in the same way as plaice.

flounder

turbot

lemon sole

halibut

dover sole

skate

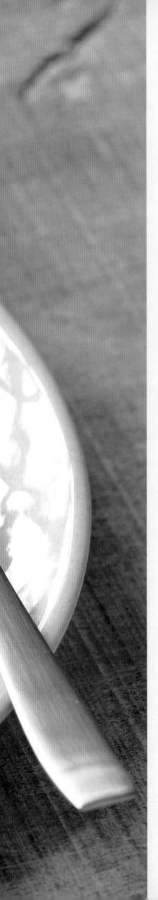

PLAICE WITH
EGG & DILL SAUCE

SERVES 4

INGREDIENTS

- 85 G/3 OZ BUTTER, PLUS EXTRA FOR GREASING
- 4 PLAICE FILLETS, EACH ABOUT 225 G/8 OZ
- JUICE OF ½ LEMON
- 4 HARD-BOILED EGGS, FINELY CHOPPED
- 4 CORNICHONS OR OTHER SMALL GHERKINS, FINELY CHOPPED
- 2 TBSP CHOPPED FRESH DILL
- SALT AND PEPPER
- FRESH DILL SPRIGS, TO GARNISH

1 Preheat the grill to medium. Generously grease a baking sheet with butter and put the fish fillets on it, skin side down.

2 Melt the butter in a saucepan over a low heat. Remove the pan from the heat and brush some of the butter over the fish. Set the remainder aside. Season the fish with salt and pepper, place under the grill and cook for 8 minutes, without turning, until the flesh flakes easily.

3 Just before the fish is cooked, stir the lemon juice, eggs, cornichons and chopped dill into the remaining melted butter. Heat gently, stirring occasionally, for 2 minutes.

4 Using a fish slice, transfer the fish fillets to warmed serving plates. Spoon over the sauce, garnish with the dill sprigs and serve immediately.

HALIBUT WITH
CARAMELIZED ONIONS

SERVES 1

INGREDIENTS

- 1 TBSP VEGETABLE OIL
- ½ SMALL ONION, THINLY SLICED
- ½ TSP BALSAMIC VINEGAR
- 1 TBSP BUTTER, MELTED
- 115 G/4 OZ HALIBUT FILLET OR HALIBUT STEAK
- SPRIGS OF FRESH FLAT-LEAF PARSLEY, TO GARNISH
- NEW POTATOES AND TOMATO QUARTERS, TO SERVE

1 Heat the oil in a large frying pan over a medium heat. Add the onion, stir well and reduce the heat. Cook for 15–20 minutes over a very low heat, stirring occasionally, until the onion is very soft and brown.

2 Add the vinegar to the pan and cook for 2 minutes, stirring constantly to prevent sticking.

3 Brush the melted butter over the fish.

4 Preheat the grill to hot. Sear the fish, then reduce the heat and cook for about 10 minutes, turning once. The cooking time will depend on the thickness of the fillet, but the fish should be firm and tender when done.

5 Remove the fish from the heat, place on a serving platter and top with the caramelized onion. Garnish with the parsley and serve with the potatoes and tomatoes.

SOLE MEUNIÈRE

SERVES 2

INGREDIENTS

- ABOUT 100 ML/3½ FL OZ MILK
- 4 TBSP PLAIN FLOUR
- 4 SOLE FILLETS, ABOUT
  175 G/6 OZ EACH, ALL DARK
  SKIN AND BONES REMOVED
- 85 G/3 OZ BUTTER
- JUICE OF ½ LEMON
- SALT AND PEPPER
- CHOPPED FRESH FLAT-LEAF
  PARSLEY, TO GARNISH
- COOKED ASPARAGUS AND
  LEMON WEDGES, TO SERVE

1 Pour the milk into a flat dish at least as large as the fillets and put the flour on a plate. Season each fillet on both sides with salt and pepper to taste.

2 Working with 1 fillet at a time, pull it very quickly through the milk, then put it in the flour, turn once to coat all over and shake off the excess flour. Continue until all the fillets are prepared.

3 Melt half the butter in a sauté pan or frying pan large enough to hold the fillets in a single layer over a medium–high heat. Add the fillets to the pan, skinned side down, and fry for 2 minutes.

4 Turn over the fillets and fry for 2–3 minutes, or until the flesh flakes easily. Transfer to warmed serving plates, skinned side up, and reserve.

5 Reduce the heat to medium and melt the remaining butter in the pan. When it stops foaming, add the lemon juice and stir, scraping the sediment from the base of the pan. Spoon the butter over the fish and sprinkle with the parsley. Serve with the asparagus and lemon wedges.

FISHERMAN'S PIE

SERVES 6

INGREDIENTS

- 900 G/2 LB WHITE FISH FILLETS, SUCH AS PLAICE, SKINNED
- 150 ML/5 FL OZ DRY WHITE WINE
- 1 TBSP CHOPPED FRESH PARSLEY, TARRAGON OR DILL
- 100 G/3½ OZ BUTTER, PLUS EXTRA FOR GREASING
- 175 G/6 OZ SMALL MUSHROOMS, SLICED
- 175 G/6 OZ COOKED PEELED PRAWNS
- 40 G/1½ OZ PLAIN FLOUR
- 125 ML/4 FL OZ DOUBLE CREAM
- 900 G/2 LB FLOURY POTATOES, SUCH AS KING EDWARD, MARIS PIPER OR DESIRÉE, PEELED AND CUT INTO CHUNKS
- SALT AND PEPPER

1 Preheat the oven to 180°C/350°F/Gas Mark 4. Grease a 1.7-litre/3-pint baking dish.

2 Fold the fish fillets in half and put in the dish. Season well with salt and pepper, pour over the wine and scatter over the parsley.

3 Cover with foil and bake in the preheated oven for 15 minutes until the fish starts to flake. Strain off the liquid and reserve for the sauce. Increase the oven temperature to 220°C/425°F/Gas Mark 7.

4 Melt 15 g/½ oz of the butter in a frying pan over a medium heat, add the mushrooms and cook, stirring frequently, for 5 minutes. Spoon over the fish. Scatter over the prawns.

5 Heat 55 g/2 oz of the remaining butter in a saucepan and stir in the flour. Cook for 3–4 minutes without browning, stirring constantly. Remove from the heat and gradually add the reserved cooking liquid, stirring well after each addition.

6 Return to the heat and slowly bring to the boil, stirring constantly, until thickened. Add the cream and season to taste with salt and pepper. Pour over the fish in the dish and smooth over the surface.

7 Bring a large saucepan of lightly salted water to the boil, add the potatoes and cook for 15–20 minutes. Drain well and mash with a potato masher until smooth. Season to taste with salt and pepper and add the remaining butter, stirring until melted.

8 Pile or pipe the potato onto the fish and sauce and bake for 10–15 minutes until golden brown.

NUT-CRUSTED
HALIBUT

SERVES 4

INGREDIENTS

- 3 TBSP BUTTER, MELTED
- 750 G/1 LB 10 OZ HALIBUT FILLET
- 55 G/2 OZ PISTACHIO NUTS, SHELLED AND VERY FINELY CHOPPED
- MIXED SALAD AND LEMON WEDGES, TO SERVE

1 Brush the melted butter over the halibut fillet.

2 Spread out the nuts on a large, flat plate. Roll the fish in the nuts, pressing down gently.

3 Preheat a griddle over a medium heat. Cook the halibut, turning once, for 10 minutes, or until firm but tender – the exact cooking time will depend on the thickness of the fillet.

4 Remove the fish and any loose pistachio pieces from the heat and transfer to a large, warmed serving platter. Serve immediately, accompanied by the mixed salad and lemon wedges.

LEMON SOLE WITH PINK PEPPERCORNS & APPLES

SERVES 4

INGREDIENTS

- 300 ML/10 FL OZ FISH STOCK (SEE PAGE 18)
- 8 LEMON SOLE FILLETS, EACH ABOUT 85 G/3 OZ, SKINNED
- 1 TBSP PINK PEPPERCORNS
- 6 TBSP CRÈME FRAÎCHE
- 3 TART GREEN EATING APPLES, CORED AND THINLY SLICED
- SALT
- SPRIGS OF FRESH FLAT-LEAF PARSLEY, TO GARNISH

1 Pour all but 3 tablespoons of the stock into a saucepan. Add the fish fillets – they usually fit better if folded in half. Bring just to the boil, then reduce the heat, cover and poach very gently for 5–8 minutes, until the flesh flakes easily.

2 Meanwhile, put the peppercorns into another saucepan with the remaining fish stock and bring to the boil over a low heat. Stir in the crème fraîche, season with salt and cook, stirring frequently, for 3–5 minutes, until reduced. Add the apples and cook for 1–2 minutes, until soft but still firm.

3 Using a fish slice, drain the fish and transfer carefully to a warmed serving plate. Using a slotted spoon, transfer the apple slices to the plate to surround the fish. Keep warm.

4 Bring the peppercorn mixture back to the boil and gradually stir in enough of the fish cooking liquid to make a sauce. Spoon the sauce over the fish and serve immediately, garnished with the parsley sprigs.

GRILLED HALIBUT WITH
GARLIC BUTTER

SERVES 4

INGREDIENTS

- 4 HALIBUT FILLETS, ABOUT 175 G/6 OZ EACH
- 6 TBSP BUTTER, PLUS EXTRA FOR GREASING
- 2 GARLIC CLOVES, FINELY CHOPPED
- SALT AND PEPPER
- SPRIGS OF FRESH FLAT-LEAF PARSLEY, TO GARNISH
- COOKED FRENCH BEANS AND LIME WEDGES, TO SERVE

1 Preheat the grill to medium. Rinse the fish fillets under cold running water, then pat dry with kitchen paper.

2 Grease a shallow, heatproof dish with butter, then arrange the fish in it. Season with salt and pepper.

3 In a separate bowl, mix the remaining butter with the garlic. Arrange pieces of the garlic butter all over the fish, then transfer to the grill. Cook for 7–8 minutes, turning once, until the fish is cooked through.

4 Remove the dish from the grill. Using a fish slice, remove the fillets from the dish and arrange on individual serving plates. Pour over the remaining melted butter from the dish, and garnish with the parsley sprigs. Serve with the French beans and lime wedges.

ROUND SEAFISH

This diverse fish family includes the oily fish salmon and tuna, which, as well as being quick and easy to prepare, are also said to reduce the risk of stroke and heart disease when eaten regularly. Whereas most seafood is overpowered by full-flavoured herbs and spices, these fish soak up the flavours to make satisfying family meals.

THE ROUND SEAFISH DIRECTORY

The following is a guide to all the main species of round seafish that can be eaten, listed by their common names, although some fish, confusingly, are known by a variety of different names. The potted profile for each fish details the various forms in which it can be purchased, for example whole or in fillets, fresh or canned, and the most suitable cooking methods.

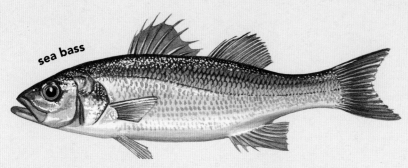

sea bass

SEA BASS/BASS

This large, sleek fish, similar in shape to the salmon, has dark, silver-grey scales, which should be removed before cooking, and a white belly. Its firm, white flesh has an excellent flavour. It can be bought whole or in cutlets or fillets and is suitable for poaching or steaming.

COD

This very popular, white-fleshed fish varies enormously in size and is available whole, which is particularly suitable for baking, poaching or steaming, and in fillets and cutlets, which can be fried or grilled. It is commonly used in cooked dishes such as Flaky Pastry Fish Pie. Much of it is frozen aboard fishing boats. It is also available salted, smoked and dried. Cod's roe is available fresh and smoked.

COLEY/SAITHE COALFISH

Coley is related to the cod family and has pinkish-grey flesh that becomes white when cooked. Usually available as fillets or cutlets, it can be used in the same way as cod but, as it can be dry, is not suitable for grilling. It is used in soups, stews and fish pies.

HOKI

Imported from New Zealand, hoki is related to hake, which, in turn, is a member of the cod family. Its white flesh is firm, contains very few bones and has a mild flavour. It is sold in fillets or pieces and can be baked, fried or grilled.

HADDOCK

This fish has a firm, white flesh and is closely related to cod, although it is usually smaller and can be distinguished by the dark streak that runs down its back and the two black marks either side of its gills. Sold as fillets or cutlets, it is interchangeable with cod in recipes and is used as an alternative when serving fish

and chips. Haddock is often smoked – it is used as such in the well known dish Kedgeree.

MONKFISH/ ANGLER FISH

This deep sea fish has such a large, ugly head that usually only the tail is sold, boned as a whole piece or skinned and filleted. The monkfish is a species that matures late and is therefore vulnerable to overfishing (see the best choices to make in the Marine Conservation Society Good Fish Guide on page 12–13).

PARROT FISH

This beautiful tropical fish, with skin ranging in colour from turquoise and green to pink and violet, and its round, beak-like face really does look like a parrot. Its flesh is white and firm and is best cooked whole.

POMFRET

This silver, fairly small fish from warm waters is a round fish but, like the John Dory, is laterally compressed and therefore prepared as though a flat fish. It is similar to butterfish, which is popular in America. The flesh is white and delicate and can be stuffed and baked whole or filleted and fried or grilled.

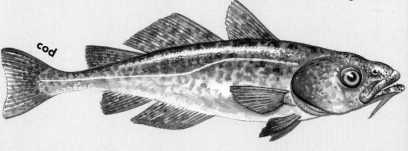

cod

RED MULLET

Red mullet, of which there are several species, is unrelated to grey mullet. It looks attractive, with its crimson skin. It has a firm, white flesh, which has a delicate flavour. Its liver, too, is considered a delicacy, which is why it is usually sold uncleaned. For this reason, it should be eaten fresh before it deteriorates. It must be scaled before cooking and is usually cooked whole, fried, grilled or baked.

SALMON

Most salmon varieties mature at sea and then return to coastal rivers and streams to spawn. Atlantic salmon (wild salmon) and farmed salmon are available, and increased harvests of farmed salmon have made this popular fish more affordable. Salmon has a high fat content and a firm flesh, which can be pink to dark red. It can be poached or baked whole and its cutlets or fillets can be fried or grilled. Its red roe is available as salmon caviar, although this description really applies only to sturgeon roe. It is also popular canned and smoked. Smoked salmon is dry-salted before being smoked and is sold in fillets, which are cut into paper-thin slices.

SALMON TROUT/ SEA TROUT

This fish is often confused with salmon as it also returns from the sea to spawn in coastal rivers. It is smaller than salmon, but larger than trout, has pale pink flesh and can be used in the same way as salmon or trout. However, it is too delicate for smoking. It can be purchased whole or as fillets.

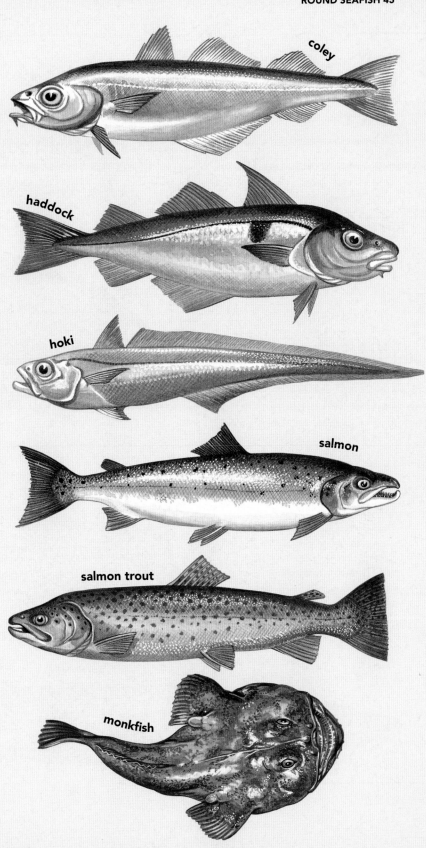

WHITING

This fish, related to hake, is fairly small and has pale brown skin and a cream belly. Its flesh is white and very soft, with a bland flavour. It can be bought fresh, either whole or in fillets, as well as smoked or salted. It is suitable for frying, grilling, poaching or steaming.

SEA BREAM

There are numerous varieties of this large fish, including the red, black, white, pink, ray and gilt-head sea bream. All have firm, white flesh, but the red bream is generally considered to have the best flavour. It is usually cooked whole and can be stuffed and baked, grilled or braised. Its interesting story is that they start life as males and later turn into females!

GREY MULLET

This fish, unrelated to the red mullet, looks and tastes similar to sea bass. It has firm, white flesh and can be bought whole or in fillets and is best baked or grilled.

BARRACUDA

This large, fierce fish from warm waters has white flesh with a firm texture. Small barracuda can be filleted and are suitable for baking, frying, grilling, poaching, steaming and for using in soups and stews. Never eat barracuda raw, or its liver, as it can be toxic.

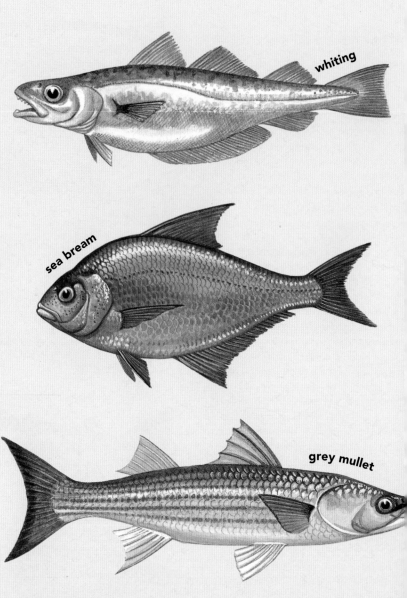

whiting

sea bream

grey mullet

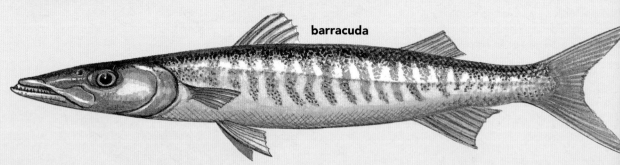

barracuda

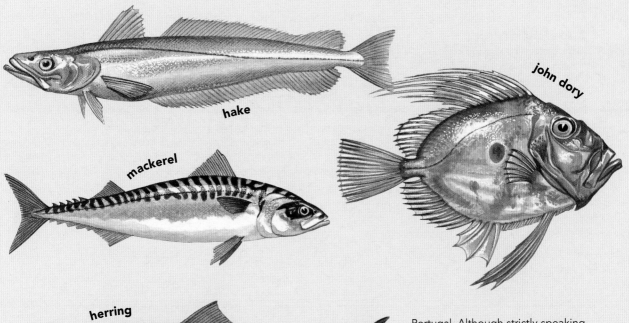

HAKE

This large fish is a member of the cod family, but has a slightly firmer, white flesh. Large hake are cut into fillets or cutlets and these are usually poached, but they can also be fried or grilled. Small hake are sold whole. Smoked hake is also available, as well as salted hake, which is prepared and used in the same way as salt cod.

HERRING

A small, very oily fish, available whole or filleted, that can be fried or grilled or stuffed and baked. Due to its oiliness, the herring is ideal for preserving. Rollmop herrings are raw herrings, boned, rolled up with chopped onions, gherkins and peppercorns and then marinated in spiced vinegar. Herrings are also smoked. Kippers are the most popular form and are sold in fillets or whole, often in pairs. Ideally, dye should not be used in the process. Buckling is another version of smoked herring, one that is often considered the best, and lightly salted bloaters and smoked herrings are also available. Herrings can be preserved between layers of salt. Canned herring is also popular.

JOHN DORY/DORY

In most parts of the world, John Dory is called St Peter or St Pierre (not to be confused with St Peter's Fish), but not in the UK, Greece or Portugal. Although strictly speaking a round fish, John Dory is laterally compressed and therefore prepared as a flat fish, from which there is little flesh and much waste. It has an ugly head with a very large jaw and a large mark on its side like a thumb print. When fresh it is golden in colour and its firm, white flesh has a delicate flavour. It is usually filleted and fried and it is also a traditional ingredient in the traditional Mediterranean fish stew bouillabaisse.

MACKEREL

This fish, with its striking black markings and silver belly, is particularly oily, which makes it ideal for frying and grilling or stuffing and baking. As its dark flesh has a distinctive flavour, it is often accompanied by a sharp-flavoured sauce, such as gooseberry. Mackerel is available whole or in fillets as well as canned or smoked. Smoked mackerel has a rich, strong flavour and is sold in fillets that are sometimes peppered or herbed to enhance the flavour of the fish.

POLLACK

Pollack is closely related to cod, although it is usually smaller and its flavour is not as good. Most is frozen aboard fishing boats. It is cooked in the same way as cod and is ideal in mixed fish soups.

RED SNAPPER

This large fish, identified by its vivid rose-pink skin and red eyes, has white, creamy flesh and is cut into fillets or cutlets, which can be fried, grilled, poached or steamed. Small ones can be stuffed and baked whole.

SARDINE/PILCHARD

These oily, strong-flavoured fish vary in size. The smaller fish are called sardines, whereas the larger, mature fish are known as pilchards, three or four of which make one serving. Sold fresh, they can be fried, grilled or baked. Canned sardines can be eaten whole as the preserving process softens their bones.

SWORDFISH

Swordfish is an enormous fish and is sold as cutlets or chunks. Its firm, dense texture makes it perfect for grilling and frying, although it can also be poached, steamed or baked.

TUNA

There are many species of this large fish, with its dark blue back and silver-grey sides and belly, including skipjack, yellowfin, bluefin, albacore and big-eye. Its flesh varies in colour from pale pink to dark red and it has a firm, dense texture. It can be bought in chunks or steaks, for frying, grilling, braising or poaching, but it should not be overcooked as it tends to dry out during cooking. Tuna is also sold canned in oil, brine or spring water.

POMPANO

This warm water fish has a silver skin and fatty flesh. It can be bought whole or in fillets. Its skin should be removed before cooking. It can be baked, fried, grilled, steamed, poached or used in soups and stews.

CONGER EEL/ MORAY EEL

These are snake-like fish whose bodies can grow up to 2.5 metres/8 feet. The conger eel was once part of the staple diet of the Cornish people, as it was easily caught along the rocky coastline of southern England. It is also available smoked. The moray eel, of which there are several species, is a cousin of the conger eel, but is much smaller. Both conger and moray eels have firm, white flesh and are usually sold in cutlets. They can be roasted or baked and are good in pies, soups and stews.

ANCHOVY

These small fish are identified by their large mouths, which almost stretch back to their gills. They are high in fat and, although occasionally available fresh, most are filleted, cured in salt and oil and then canned. They are sold flat or rolled.

LING

Ling, with its long, brown, eel-like body, is the largest member of the cod family and has soft, white flesh. It is seldom available fresh, but is usually either salted or smoked.

SPRAT

Sprat is now rarely sold fresh, but is available smoked. It is very similar to a small herring and can be used in the same way.

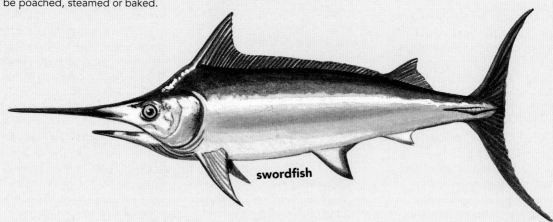

swordfish

red snapper

sardine

pompano

anchovy

tuna

HADDOCK & POTATO SOUP

SERVES 4

INGREDIENTS

- 2 TBSP BUTTER
- 1 ONION, CHOPPED
- 1 LEEK, CHOPPED
- 2 TBSP PLAIN FLOUR
- 850 ML/1½ PINTS MILK
- 1 BAY LEAF
- 2 TBSP CHOPPED FRESH PARSLEY, PLUS EXTRA TO GARNISH
- 350 G/12 OZ SMOKED HADDOCK FILLETS, SKINNED
- 450 G/1 LB POTATOES, COOKED AND MASHED
- 6 TBSP DOUBLE CREAM
- SALT AND PEPPER
- FRESH CRUSTY ROLLS, TO SERVE

1 Melt the butter in a large saucepan over a medium heat, add the onion and leek and cook, stirring frequently, for 3 minutes, or until slightly soft. Mix the flour in a bowl with enough of the milk to make a smooth paste, then stir into the saucepan. Cook, stirring constantly, for 2 minutes, then gradually stir in the remaining milk. Add the bay leaf and parsley and season to taste with salt and pepper. Bring to the boil, then reduce the heat and simmer for 15 minutes.

2 Rinse the haddock fillets under cold running water, drain, then cut into bite-sized chunks. Add to the soup and cook for 15 minutes, or until the fish is tender and cooked right through. Add the mashed potatoes and stir in the cream. Cook for a further 2–3 minutes, then remove from the heat and remove and discard the bay leaf.

3 Ladle into warmed serving bowls, garnish with chopped parsley and serve with crusty rolls.

SMOKED COD
CHOWDER

SERVES 4

INGREDIENTS

- 25 G/1 OZ BUTTER
- 1 ONION, FINELY CHOPPED
- 1 SMALL CELERY STICK, FINELY DICED
- 250 G/9 OZ POTATOES, DICED
- 55 G/2 OZ CARROTS, DICED
- 300 ML/10 FL OZ BOILING WATER
- 350 G/12 OZ SMOKED COD FILLETS, SKINNED AND CUT INTO BITE-SIZED PIECES
- 300 ML/10 FL OZ MILK
- SALT AND PEPPER
- FRESH FLAT-LEAF PARSLEY SPRIGS, TO GARNISH

1 Melt the butter in a large saucepan over a low heat, add the onion and celery and cook, stirring frequently, for 5 minutes, or until soft but not brown.

2 Add the potatoes, carrots, water and salt and pepper to taste. Bring to the boil, then reduce the heat and simmer for 10 minutes, or until the vegetables are tender. Add the fish to the chowder and cook for a further 10 minutes.

3 Pour in the milk and heat gently. Taste and adjust the seasoning, if necessary. Serve hot, in warmed soup bowls, garnished with the parsley sprigs.

ROASTED SALMON WITH
LEMON & HERBS

SERVES 4

INGREDIENTS

- 6 TBSP EXTRA VIRGIN OLIVE OIL
- 1 ONION, SLICED
- 1 LEEK, TRIMMED AND SLICED
- JUICE OF ½ LEMON
- 2 TBSP CHOPPED FRESH
  PARSLEY
- 2 TBSP CHOPPED FRESH DILL
- 500 G/1 LB 2 OZ SALMON
  FILLETS
- SALT AND PEPPER
- FRESHLY COOKED BABY
  SPINACH LEAVES AND LEMON
  WEDGES, TO SERVE

1 Preheat the oven to 200°C/400°F/Gas Mark 6. Heat 1 tablespoon of the oil in a frying pan over a medium heat. Add the onion and leek and cook, stirring, for about 4 minutes until slightly soft.

2 Meanwhile, put the remaining oil in a small bowl with the lemon juice and herbs, and season. Stir together well. Rinse the fish under cold running water, then pat dry with kitchen paper. Arrange the fish in a shallow, ovenproof baking dish.

3 Remove the frying pan from the heat and spread the onion and leek over the fish. Pour the oil mixture over the top, ensuring that everything is well coated. Roast in the centre of the preheated oven for about 10 minutes or until the fish is cooked through.

4 Arrange the cooked spinach on warmed serving plates. Remove the fish and vegetables from the oven and arrange on top of the spinach. Serve immediately, accompanied by the lemon wedges.

TUNA WITH GREEN SAUCE

SERVES 4

INGREDIENTS

- 4 FRESH TUNA STEAKS, ABOUT
  2 CM/¾ INCH THICK
- OLIVE OIL, FOR BRUSHING
- SALT AND PEPPER
- LEMON WEDGES, TO SERVE

GREEN SAUCE

- 55 G/2 OZ FRESH FLAT-LEAF
  PARSLEY, LEAVES AND STEMS
- 4 SPRING ONIONS, CHOPPED
- 2 GARLIC CLOVES, CHOPPED
- 3 ANCHOVY FILLETS IN OIL,
  DRAINED
- 30 G/1 OZ FRESH BASIL LEAVES
- ½ TBSP CAPERS IN BRINE,
  RINSED AND DRIED
- 2 SPRIGS OF FRESH OREGANO
  OR ½ TSP DRIED OREGANO
- 125 ML/4 FL OZ EXTRA VIRGIN
  OLIVE OIL
- 1–2 TBSP LEMON JUICE,
  TO TASTE

1 To make the green sauce, put the parsley, spring onions, garlic, anchovy fillets, basil, capers and oregano in a food processor. Pulse to chop and blend together. With the motor still running, pour in the oil through the feed tube. Add lemon juice to taste, then whiz again. If the sauce is too thick, add a little extra oil. Cover and chill until required.

2 Place a cast-iron griddle pan over a high heat until you can feel the heat rising from the surface. Brush the tuna steaks with oil and place, oiled side down, on the hot pan and cook for 2 minutes.

3 Lightly brush the top side of the tuna steaks with a little more oil. Use a pair of tongs to turn over the tuna steaks, then season to taste with salt and pepper. Continue cooking for a further 2 minutes for rare or for up to 4 minutes for well done.

4 Transfer the tuna steaks to serving plates and serve with the green sauce spooned over, accompanied by the lemon wedges.

BAKED LEMON COD WITH HERB SAUCE

SERVES 4

INGREDIENTS

- 4 THICK COD FILLETS
- OLIVE OIL, FOR BRUSHING
- 8 THIN LEMON SLICES
- SALT AND PEPPER
- COOKED FRENCH BEANS, TO SERVE

HERB SAUCE

- 4 TBSP OLIVE OIL
- 1 GARLIC CLOVE, CRUSHED
- 4 TBSP CHOPPED FRESH PARSLEY
- 2 TBSP CHOPPED FRESH MINT
- JUICE OF ½ LEMON
- SALT AND PEPPER

1 Preheat the oven to 200°C/400°F/Gas Mark 6. Rinse each cod fillet and pat dry with kitchen paper, then brush with oil. Place each fillet on a piece of baking paper large enough to encase the fish in a parcel. Top each fillet with 2 lemon slices and season to taste with salt and pepper. Fold over the baking paper to encase the fish and bake in the preheated oven for 20 minutes, or until just cooked and opaque.

2 Meanwhile, to make the herb sauce, put all the ingredients into a food processor and process until finely chopped. Season to taste with salt and pepper.

3 Carefully unfold each parcel and place on a serving plate. Pour a spoonful of herb sauce over each piece of fish before serving, accompanied by the French beans.

GRILLED SWORDFISH WITH CORIANDER-LIME BUTTER

SERVES 4

INGREDIENTS

- CORN OIL, FOR BRUSHING
- 4 SWORDFISH STEAKS, ABOUT
  175 G/6 OZ EACH AND
  2.5 CM/1 INCH THICK
- SALT AND PEPPER
- FRESH CORIANDER LEAVES,
  TO GARNISH
- CHERRY TOMATOES, TO SERVE

CORIANDER-LIME BUTTER

- 125 G/4½ OZ UNSALTED BUTTER,
  SOFTENED
- FINELY GRATED RIND OF
  1 LARGE LIME
- ¼ TSP FRESHLY SQUEEZED
  LIME JUICE
- 1 TBSP VERY FINELY SHREDDED
  CORIANDER LEAVES
- PINCH OF GROUND CUMIN

1 To make the coriander-lime butter, put the butter into a bowl and beat until it is soft and smooth. Stir in the lime rind, lime juice, shredded coriander, cumin, and salt and pepper to taste. Spoon the butter onto a piece of greaseproof paper and roll into a log about 3 cm/1¼ inches thick. Refrigerate for at least 45 minutes or freeze until required.

2 When ready to cook the swordfish steaks, preheat the grill to high. Brush the grill rack with a little oil and position it about 10 cm/4 inches below the heat source.

3 Brush the steaks with oil and season to taste with salt and pepper. Put the steaks on the grill rack and cook for 4 minutes. Turn them over, then brush with a little more oil, season to taste with salt and pepper, and cook for a further 4–5 minutes, or until the fish is cooked and the flesh flakes easily.

4 Meanwhile, cut the butter into 8 equal slices. Put 2 slices of the butter on top of each steak and serve at once, garnished with the coriander leaves, accompanied by the cherry tomatoes.

TERIYAKI SALMON FILLETS WITH CHINESE NOODLES

SERVES 4

INGREDIENTS

- 4 SALMON FILLETS, ABOUT 200 G/7 OZ EACH
- 125 ML/4 FL OZ TERIYAKI MARINADE
- 1 SHALLOT, SLICED
- 2-CM/¾-INCH PIECE FRESH GINGER, FINELY CHOPPED
- 2 CARROTS, SLICED
- 115 G/4 OZ CLOSED-CUP MUSHROOMS, SLICED
- 1.2 LITRES/2 PINTS VEGETABLE STOCK
- 250 G/9 OZ DRIED MEDIUM EGG NOODLES
- 115 G/4 OZ FROZEN PEAS
- 175 G/6 OZ CHINESE LEAVES, SHREDDED
- 4 SPRING ONIONS, SLICED

1 Wipe off any fish scales from the salmon skin. Arrange the salmon fillets, skin side up, in a dish just large enough to fit them in a single layer. Mix the teriyaki marinade with the shallot and ginger in a small bowl and pour over the salmon. Cover and leave to marinate in the refrigerator for at least 1 hour, turning the salmon over halfway through the marinating time.

2 Put the carrots, mushrooms and stock into a large saucepan. Arrange the salmon, skin side down, on a shallow baking tray. Pour the fish marinade into the pan of vegetables and stock and bring to the boil. Reduce the heat, cover and simmer for 10 minutes.

3 Meanwhile, preheat the grill to medium. Cook the salmon under the preheated grill for 10–15 minutes, depending on the thickness of the fillets, until the flesh turns pink and flakes easily. Remove from under the grill and keep warm.

4 Add the noodles and peas to the stock and return to the boil. Reduce the heat, cover and simmer for 5 minutes, or until the noodles are tender. Stir in the Chinese leaves and spring onions and heat through for 1 minute.

5 Carefully drain off 300 ml/10 fl oz of the stock into a small heatproof jug and reserve. Drain and discard the remaining stock. Divide the noodles and vegetables between 4 warmed serving bowls and top each with a salmon fillet. Pour the reserved stock over each meal and serve immediately.

SWEET & SOUR SEA BASS

SERVES 2

INGREDIENTS

- 60 G/2¼ OZ PAK CHOI, SHREDDED
- 40 G/1½ OZ BEANSPROUTS
- 40 G/1½ OZ SHIITAKE MUSHROOMS, SLICED
- 40 G/1½ OZ OYSTER MUSHROOMS, TORN
- 20 G/¾ OZ SPRING ONION, FINELY SLICED
- 1 TSP FINELY GRATED FRESH GINGER
- 1 TBSP FINELY SLICED LEMON GRASS
- 2 X 90 G/3¼ OZ SEA BASS FILLETS, SKINNED AND BONED
- 10 G/¼ OZ SESAME SEEDS, TOASTED

SWEET & SOUR SAUCE

- 90 ML/3 FL OZ UNSWEETENED PINEAPPLE JUICE
- 1 TBSP SUGAR
- 1 TBSP RED WINE VINEGAR
- 2 STAR ANISE, CRUSHED
- 90 ML/3 FL OZ TOMATO JUICE
- 1 TBSP CORNFLOUR, BLENDED WITH A LITTLE COLD WATER

1 Preheat the oven to 200°C/400°F/Gas Mark 6. Cut out two 38-cm/15-inch squares of greaseproof paper and two 38-cm/15-inch squares of foil.

2 To make the sauce, heat the pineapple juice, sugar, red wine vinegar, star anise and tomato juice and simmer for 1–2 minutes. Thicken with the cornflour and water mixture, whisking constantly, then pass through a fine sieve into a small bowl to cool.

3 In a separate large bowl mix together the pak choi, beansprouts, mushrooms and spring onions, then add the ginger and lemon grass. Toss all the ingredients together.

4 Put a square of greaseproof paper on top of a square of foil and fold into a triangle. Open up and place half the vegetable mix in the centre, pour half the sweet and sour sauce over the vegetables and place the sea bass on top. Sprinkle with a few sesame seeds. Close the triangle over the mixture and, starting at the top, fold the right corner and crumple the edges together to form an airtight triangular bag. Repeat to make the second bag.

5 Place the foil bags on a baking tray and cook in the oven for 10 minutes until they puff with steam. To serve, place the bags on individual plates and snip them open at the table so that you can enjoy the wonderful aromas as they are opened.

FLAKY PASTRY FISH PIE

SERVES 4–6

INGREDIENTS

- 650 G/1 LB 7 OZ WHITE FISH FILLETS, SUCH AS COD OR HADDOCK, SKINNED
- 300 ML/10 FL OZ MILK
- 1 BAY LEAF
- 4 PEPPERCORNS
- 1 SMALL ONION, FINELY SLICED
- 40 G/1½ OZ BUTTER, PLUS EXTRA FOR GREASING
- 40 G/1½ OZ PLAIN FLOUR, PLUS EXTRA FOR DUSTING
- 1 TBSP CHOPPED FRESH PARSLEY OR TARRAGON
- 150 ML/5 FL OZ SINGLE CREAM
- 2 HARD-BOILED EGGS, ROUGHLY CHOPPED
- 400 G/14 OZ READY-MADE PUFF PASTRY
- 1 EGG, BEATEN
- SALT AND PEPPER

1 Preheat the oven to 200°C/400°F/Gas Mark 6. Grease a 1.2-litre/2-pint pie dish.

2 Put the fish in a frying pan and cover with the milk. Add the bay leaf, peppercorns and onion slices. Bring to the boil, then reduce the heat and simmer gently for 10–12 minutes.

3 Remove from the heat and strain off the milk into a measuring jug. Add a little extra milk, if necessary, to make up to 300 ml/10 fl oz. Flake the fish into large pieces, removing and discarding any bones.

4 Melt the butter in a saucepan over a low heat, add the flour and cook, stirring constantly, for 2–3 minutes. Remove from the heat and gradually stir in the reserved milk, beating well after each addition. Return the saucepan to the heat and cook, stirring constantly, until thickened. Cook for a further 2–3 minutes until smooth and glossy. Add the herbs, cream, and salt and pepper to taste.

5 Put the fish in the pie dish, then add the hard-boiled eggs and season to taste with salt and pepper. Pour the sauce over the fish and mix carefully.

6 Roll out the pastry on a lightly floured work surface until just larger than the pie dish. Cut off a strip 1 cm/½ inch wide from around the edge. Moisten the rim of the dish with water and press the pastry strip onto it. Moisten the pastry collar and put on the pastry lid. Crimp the edges to seal well. If desired, garnish with the pastry trimmings shaped into leaves. Brush with the beaten egg.

7 Put the pie on a baking tray and bake near the top of the preheated oven for 20–25 minutes. Cover with foil if it begins to get too brown.

FISH & CHIPS

SERVES 2

INGREDIENTS

- VEGETABLE OIL, FOR DEEP-FRYING
- 3 LARGE POTATOES, SUCH AS CARA OR DESIRÉE
- 2 THICK COD OR HADDOCK FILLETS, 175 G/6 OZ EACH
- 175 G/6 OZ SELF-RAISING FLOUR, PLUS EXTRA FOR DUSTING
- 200 ML/7 FL OZ COLD LAGER
- SALT AND PEPPER
- SPRIGS OF FRESH FLAT-LEAF PARSLEY, TO GARNISH
- TARTARE SAUCE, TO SERVE (SEE PAGE 20)

1 Heat the oil in a temperature-controlled deep-fat fryer to 120°C/250°F, or in a heavy-based saucepan, checking the temperature with a thermometer, to blanch the chips. Preheat the oven to 150°C/300°F/Gas Mark 2.

2 Peel the potatoes and cut into even-sized chips. Fry for about 8–10 minutes, depending on size, until soft but not coloured. Remove from the oil, drain on kitchen paper and place in a warm dish in the preheated oven. Increase the temperature of the oil to 180°C/350°F, or until a cube of bread browns in 30 seconds.

3 Meanwhile, season the fish with salt and pepper and dust it lightly with a little flour.

4 Make a thick batter by sifting the flour into a bowl with a little salt and whisking in most of the lager. Check the consistency before adding the remainder: it should be very thick like double cream.

5 Dip one fillet into the batter and allow the batter to coat it thickly. Carefully place the fish in the hot oil, then repeat with the other fillet.

6 Cook for 8–10 minutes, depending on the thickness of the fish. Turn the fillets over halfway through the cooking time. Remove the fish from the fryer, drain and keep warm.

7 Make sure the oil temperature is still at 180°C/350°F and return the chips to the fryer. Cook for a further 2–3 minutes until golden brown and crispy. Drain and season with salt and pepper before serving with the battered fish and some Tartare Sauce, garnished with parsley.

FRESHWATER FISH

When you're in the mood for something different, give freshwater fish a try. Freshwater fish are best known for their mild, delicate flavour and the flesh varies from fine to coarse, depending on the species. The skin and a thin layer of fat are often removed before cooking, and these fish are good baked, fried or poached.

THE FRESHWATER FISH DIRECTORY

The following is a guide to all the main species of freshwater fish that can be eaten, listed by their common names, although some fish, confusingly, are known by a variety of different names. The potted profile for each fish details the various forms in which it can be purchased, for example whole or in fillets, fresh or canned, and the most suitable cooking methods.

CATFISH/ROCKFISH

There are many species of catfish, many of which are frozen. It is available whole or as fillets and its tough skin must be removed before cooking. It can be fried, grilled, poached, steamed, baked or used in soups and stews.

TROUT

There are many varieties of trout, including river, brown, rainbow and salmon trout. It is usually cooked whole and can be baked, fried, grilled, poached or steamed. It is also available smoked, in the same way as smoked salmon.

CHAR

Char is similar to trout in size and appearance, but more colourful. Its flesh is firm and usually white, or sometimes pale pink. Arctic char is now commonly available, thanks to farming in Iceland and Canada. It is usually sold filleted and can be fried, baked or steamed.

TILAPIA/ST PETER'S FISH

Farming has made tilapia more widely available and it can now be purchased whole or as fillets. It has a firm texture and is suitable for all cooking methods. An interesting feature of this fish is that the females carry their young in their mouths. They are smaller than the males.

trout

catfish

EEL/COMMON EEL/ ELVER

This snake-like fish, smaller than the seawater conger eel, lives in rivers and streams and then swims thousands of kilometres to return to the sea and spawn, after which it dies (the opposite migratory habit of salmon). Elvers are baby eels and are no longer eaten, but used to restock fisheries. Eels are currently overfished and should be avoided at the present time.

eel

Preparing a fish noisette from a fish cutlet

1 After removing the pinbones, using a sharp knife, remove the skin from the flesh halfway around the cutlet.

2 Curl the skinned piece of fish into the centre and wrap the rest of the cutlet around the outside.

3 Wrap the loose piece of skin around the cutlet and secure the whole noisette with wooden cocktail sticks.

TROUT WITH MUSSELS & PRAWNS

SERVES 4

INGREDIENTS

- 30 G/1 OZ BUTTER
- ½ TBSP SUNFLOWER OIL
- 12 BUTTON MUSHROOMS, THINLY SLICED
- 24 LIVE MUSSELS
- 1 SHALLOT, CHOPPED
- 1 GARLIC CLOVE, CRUSHED
- 250 ML/9 FL OZ DRY WHITE WINE
- 24 RAW PRAWNS IN THEIR SHELLS
- 4 TROUT FILLETS, ABOUT 175 G/6 OZ EACH, ALL SKIN AND BONES REMOVED
- 250 ML/9 FL OZ DOUBLE CREAM
- SALT AND PEPPER
- SPRIGS OF FRESH CHERVIL, TO GARNISH

BEURRE MANIÉ
- 15 G/½ OZ UNSALTED BUTTER, SOFTENED
- 15 G/½ OZ PLAIN FLOUR

1 Melt the butter with the oil in a heavy-based frying pan over a medium–high heat. Add the mushrooms and sauté for 5–7 minutes until brown, then set aside.

2 Meanwhile, preheat the oven to 190°C/375°F/Gas Mark 5. Lightly grease an ovenproof dish large enough to hold the trout fillets in a single layer and set aside.

3 To prepare the mussels, cut off and discard any beards, then scrub any dirty shells. Discard any mussels with broken shells or open ones that do not instantly close when tapped.

4 Put the shallot, garlic and wine in a large saucepan with a tight-fitting lid over a high heat and bring to the boil. Reduce the heat to very low. Add the mussels and prawns to the saucepan, cover tightly and simmer for 4 minutes, shaking the pan frequently, or until the mussels open and the prawns turn pink. Discard any mussels that do not open.

5 Line a large sieve with a piece of muslin and place over a large bowl. Tip the contents of the pan into the sieve and strain, reserving the cooking liquid.

6 Remove the mussels from their shells, reserving 4 unshelled mussels for a garnish. Peel the prawns and reserve the shells and heads, then set aside the mussels and prawns.

7 Put the cooking liquid in a small saucepan over a high heat, add the prawn shells and heads and boil for 3 minutes, skimming the surface if necessary.

8 Lay the trout fillets in the prepared dish and strain the cooking juices over. Sprinkle with the sliced mushrooms. Cover the dish with foil, shiny side down, and bake for 10–12 minutes until the trout is tender and flakes easily. Remove the trout, add to the shellfish and cover to keep warm, reserving the cooking liquid.

9 Meanwhile, to make the Beurre Manié, mash the butter and flour together to make a thick paste.

10 To make the sauce, pour the cooking liquid into a small saucepan over a high heat. Bring to the boil, then add small amounts of the Beurre Manié, whisking constantly and adding more only when the previous amount has been incorporated. Continue boiling and whisking until the sauce is thick and shiny. Stir in the cream and boil until the sauce has reduced by half. Add salt and pepper to taste, then stir in the mussels and prawns and just warm through.

11 Transfer the trout fillets to warmed plates and spoon the sauce and shellfish over. Garnish with the chervil and the reserved unshelled mussels.

CREAMY SMOKED TROUT TAGLIATELLE

SERVES 6

INGREDIENTS

- 2 CARROTS, CUT INTO THIN BATONS
- 2 CELERY STICKS, CUT INTO THIN BATONS
- 1 COURGETTE, CUT INTO THIN BATONS
- 1 LEEK, CUT INTO THIN BATONS
- 115 G/4 OZ FRESH OR FROZEN PEAS
- 150 ML/5 FL OZ VEGETABLE STOCK
- 225 G/8 OZ SMOKED TROUT FILLETS, SKINNED AND CUT INTO THIN STRIPS
- 200 G/7 OZ CREAM CHEESE
- 150 ML/5 FL OZ DRY WHITE WINE
- 2 TBSP CHOPPED FRESH DILL, PLUS EXTRA SPRIGS TO GARNISH
- 225 G/8 OZ DRIED TAGLIATELLE
- SALT AND PEPPER

1 Put the carrots, celery, courgette, leek and peas in a large, heavy-based saucepan and pour in the stock. Bring to the boil, then reduce the heat and simmer for 5 minutes, or until the vegetables are tender and most of the stock has evaporated. Remove the pan from the heat, stir in the smoked trout and cover to keep warm.

2 Put the cheese and wine in a separate large, heavy-based saucepan over a low heat and stir until the cheese has melted and the mixture is smooth. Stir in the chopped dill and season to taste with salt and pepper.

3 Meanwhile, bring another large, heavy-based saucepan of lightly salted water to the boil. Add the pasta, return to the boil and cook for 8–10 minutes, until the pasta is tender but still firm to the bite. Drain the pasta and tip into the cheese sauce. Toss the pasta using 2 large forks, then transfer to a warmed serving dish. Top with the smoked trout mixture, garnish with the dill sprigs and serve immediately.

GRILLED MUSHROOM & SPINACH-STUFFED TROUT

SERVES 2

INGREDIENTS

- 2 WHOLE TROUT, ABOUT 350 G/12 OZ EACH, GUTTED
- 1 TBSP VEGETABLE OIL
- SALT AND PEPPER

STUFFING

- 25 G/1 OZ BUTTER
- 2 SHALLOTS, FINELY CHOPPED
- 55 G/2 OZ MUSHROOMS, FINELY CHOPPED
- 55 G/2 OZ BABY SPINACH
- 1 TBSP CHOPPED FRESH PARSLEY OR TARRAGON
- GRATED RIND OF 1 LEMON
- WHOLE NUTMEG, FOR GRATING

TOMATO SALSA

- 2 TOMATOES, PEELED, DESEEDED AND FINELY DICED
- 10-CM/4-INCH PIECE OF CUCUMBER, FINELY DICED
- 2 SPRING ONIONS, FINELY CHOPPED
- 1 TBSP OLIVE OIL
- SALT AND PEPPER

1 Clean the trout, trim the fins with a pair of scissors and wipe the inside of the fish with kitchen paper. Leave the head and tail on and slash the skin of each fish on both sides about 5 times. Brush with the oil and season well with salt and pepper, both inside and out.

2 To make the stuffing, melt the butter in a small saucepan and gently soften the shallots for 2–3 minutes. Add the mushrooms and continue to cook for a further 2 minutes. Add the spinach and heat until it is just wilted.

3 Remove from the heat and add the herbs, lemon rind and a good grating of nutmeg. Allow to cool.

4 Fill the trout with the mushroom and spinach stuffing, then reshape them as neatly as you can.

5 Grill the trout under a medium grill for 10–12 minutes, turning once. The skin should be brown and crispy. Alternatively, barbecue for 6–8 minutes on each side, depending on the heat.

6 To make the tomato salsa, mix all the ingredients together and season well with the salt and pepper.

7 Serve the trout hot, with the tomato salsa spooned over them.

TROUT WITH DRIED FRUIT SAUCE

SERVES 6

INGREDIENTS

- 2 ONIONS, SLICED
- 1 GARLIC CLOVE, FINELY CHOPPED
- 2 CELERY STICKS, SLICED
- 1 CARROT, CHOPPED
- 1 TSP GROUND CUMIN
- 1 TSP GROUND ALLSPICE
- 1 BAY LEAF
- 6 CLOVES
- 6 BLACK PEPPERCORNS
- 225 ML/8 FL OZ WHITE WINE VINEGAR
- 125 ML/4 FL OZ BEER
- 6 TROUT OR CARP STEAKS OR CUTLETS, EACH 175–225 G/ 6–8 OZ
- 25 G/1 OZ BUTTER
- 175 G/6 OZ READY-TO-EAT PRUNES, CHOPPED
- 55 G/2 OZ RAISINS
- 55 G/2 OZ WALNUTS, FINELY CHOPPED
- 1 TBSP BROWN SUGAR
- GRATED RIND AND JUICE OF 1 LEMON
- SALAD LEAVES AND LIME WEDGES, TO SERVE

1 Put the onions, garlic, celery, carrot, cumin, allspice, bay leaf, cloves and peppercorns in a large saucepan and pour in the vinegar, beer and 850 ml/1½ pints of water. Bring to the boil over a medium heat, then reduce the heat, cover and simmer for 30 minutes.

2 Add the fish to the pan, re-cover and simmer for a further 30 minutes, until the flesh flakes easily.

3 Just before the fish is ready, melt the butter in a saucepan. Stir in the prunes, raisins, walnuts, sugar and lemon rind and juice and simmer gently.

4 Using a fish slice, transfer the fish to a warmed serving dish and keep warm. Strain the cooking liquid and discard the vegetables. Measure 450 ml/15 fl oz of the cooking liquid and stir it into the prune and raisin mixture. Cook over a low heat, stirring frequently, for 5 minutes, until heated through. Spoon the sauce over the fish and serve immediately with the salad leaves and lime wedges.

SHELLFISH

Once considered a luxurious treat, large stocks of farmed shellfish mean that they are now much more affordable, which is a real bonus for busy cooks. Oysters and clams can be enjoyed raw, but the hallmark of successful shellfish dishes is simple, quick cooking – take care not to overcook or the texture becomes tough. If the idea of Lobster Cooked Beach Style seems too challenging, start off with the familiar Prawn Cocktail.

THE SHELLFISH DIRECTORY

The following is a guide to all the main species of edible shellfish, listed by their common names, although some are known by a variety of different names. The potted profile for each fish details the various forms in which it can be purchased, for example live or cooked, fresh or canned, frozen or smoked, and the most suitable cooking methods.

CLAM

There are many varieties of clam, which vary in size and have either soft or hard shells. They are sold live in their shells and larger clams are steamed open, whereas smaller varieties can be eaten raw. They are also sold smoked and canned.

MUSSEL

Identified by their dark blue shell, mussels cling to rocks or the sea bed and take about two years to reach maturity. They are available live or frozen and are cooked by steaming, which opens their shells. The best known mussels recipe is Moules Marinière.

OYSTER

There are many varieties of this shellfish, which vary in size. The traditional way of eating them is raw, straight from the half shell, with their juices. Shucked (shelled) oysters are available smoked, canned and dried.

SCALLOP AND QUEEN

Scallops and queens both have ribbed fan shells, but queen scallops, or queenies, are smaller than scallops and are more widely available. Unlike other molluscs, scallops cannot hold their shells tightly closed and die soon after they are taken out of water. This means that they are very perishable and are often removed from their shells and iced aboard fishing boats as soon as they are caught. Both the white muscle and orange coral, or roe, are eaten and have an exquisite, delicate taste. They can be bought fresh or frozen and can be fried, grilled or steamed.

SHRIMP

This is the smallest crustacean, of which there are several varieties, such as the brown, pink and deep-water shrimp. Like prawns, they are translucent when alive and turn pink when cooked. Shrimps are mainly sold frozen, but are also available canned, salted and dried.

PRAWN

This shellfish is larger than the shrimp and is also available cooked whole or peeled and frozen, canned or dried. A classic way of serving prawns as a starter is Prawn Cocktail.

clam

prawn

mussel

scallop

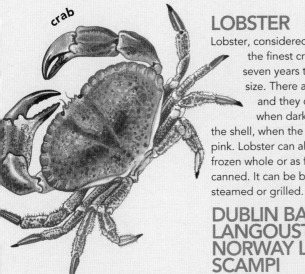

crab

CRAB

There are several varieties of this crustacean, including the blue or soft-shell crab, the common crab, the green or shore crab and the spider crab. Crab can be bought live, uncooked in the shell, cooked, with or without the shell, fresh and canned. Its flesh consists of white meat, found in the claws and legs, and brown meat, found in the body. Crab can be baked, steamed or boiled. Fresh crab can also be purchased 'dressed', with the meat arranged attractively in the shell ready for eating. Canned dressed crab is also available.

LOBSTER

Lobster, considered by some to be the finest crustacean, can take seven years to reach marketable size. There are several varieties and they can be bought live, when dark blue, or cooked in the shell, when the lobster turns bright pink. Lobster can also be purchased frozen whole or as frozen tails, and canned. It can be baked, boiled, steamed or grilled.

DUBLIN BAY PRAWN/ LANGOUSTINE/ NORWAY LOBSTER/ SCAMPI

This attractive shellfish looks like a miniature version of a lobster. It is available live or cooked, with its shell or peeled. When peeled and coated in breadcrumbs, it is known as scampi.

ROCK LOBSTER/ SPINY LOBSTER

This is another shellfish that looks similar to a small lobster. It is prepared and cooked in the same way as lobster.

FRESHWATER CRAYFISH

Also resembling a tiny lobster, these are the only shellfish found in fresh waters.

OCTOPUS

The octopus is a cephalopod and has eight tentacles. It varies in size and large ones – as large as 3 metres/10 feet – are available prepared in pieces and small ones are available whole. Octopus can be poached or used in soups and stews.

SQUID

The squid, of which there are several varieties varying in size, is a cephalopod and has ten tentacles. The tentacles are chopped and the body either sliced or kept whole and stuffed. Large squid are usually stewed and small squid can be fried, grilled or poached. The ink, found in a sac, can also be used in cooking. Squid is available fresh or frozen.

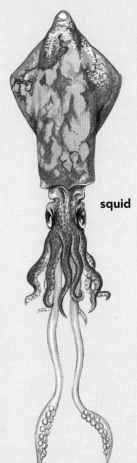

squid

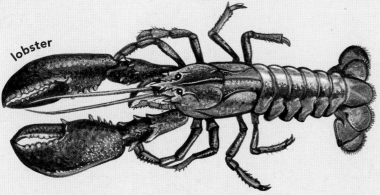

lobster

SEAFOOD & BASIL SOUP

SERVES 4

INGREDIENTS

- 2 TBSP VEGETABLE OR GROUNDNUT OIL
- 4 SHALLOTS, FINELY CHOPPED
- 2 GARLIC CLOVES, CHOPPED
- 2 TSP GROUND TURMERIC
- 2 LEMON GRASS STALKS, SNAPPED INTO THREE PIECES
- 2 FRESH GREEN CHILLIES, DESEEDED AND SLICED
- 3 CORIANDER SPRIGS, CHOPPED
- 3 LARGE TOMATOES, PEELED, DESEEDED AND CHOPPED, OR 400 G/14 OZ CANNED TOMATOES, CHOPPED
- 850 ML/1½ PINTS FISH STOCK
- 2 TSP PALM SUGAR OR SOFT, LIGHT BROWN SUGAR
- 2 TBSP FISH SAUCE
- 225 G/8 OZ LIVE MUSSELS
- 12 UNCOOKED KING PRAWNS, PEELED, WITH TAILS LEFT INTACT
- 225 G/8 OZ WHITE FISH FILLET, SKINNED AND CUT INTO LARGE CUBES
- 225 G/8 OZ SQUID, CUT INTO RINGS
- JUICE OF 1 LIME
- 3–4 SPRIGS FRESH THAI BASIL, TO GARNISH

1 Heat the oil in a wok or large frying pan and stir-fry the shallots, garlic, turmeric, lemon grass, chillies and coriander for 1–2 minutes to release the flavours.

2 Add the chopped tomatoes, stock, sugar and fish sauce and simmer for 8–10 minutes.

3 Scrub the mussels under cold running water and tug off the beards. Discard any with broken or damaged shells and those that do not shut immediately when sharply tapped.

4 Add the prawns, mussels, white fish cubes and squid to the wok, cover and simmer for 3–5 minutes, until the fish is cooked and the mussels have opened. Discard any mussels that remain closed. Stir in the lime juice, ladle into warmed bowls, garnish with the Thai basil leaves and serve immediately.

PRAWN COCKTAIL

SERVES 4

INGREDIENTS

- ½ WEBBS LETTUCE, FINELY SHREDDED
- 150 ML/5 FL OZ MAYONNAISE
- 2 TBSP SINGLE CREAM
- 2 TBSP TOMATO KETCHUP
- FEW DROPS OF TABASCO SAUCE, OR TO TASTE
- JUICE OF ½ LEMON, OR TO TASTE
- 175 G/6 OZ COOKED PEELED PRAWNS
- SALT AND PEPPER
- THINLY SLICED BUTTERED BROWN BREAD, TO SERVE (OPTIONAL)

TO GARNISH

- PAPRIKA, FOR SPRINKLING
- 4 COOKED PRAWNS, IN THEIR SHELLS
- 4 LEMON SLICES

1 Divide the lettuce between 4 small serving dishes (traditionally, stemmed glass ones, but any small dishes will be fine).

2 Mix the mayonnaise, cream and tomato ketchup together in a bowl. Add the Tabasco sauce and lemon juice and season well with salt and pepper.

3 Divide the prawns equally between the dishes and pour over the dressing. Cover and leave to chill in the refrigerator for 30 minutes.

4 Sprinkle a little paprika over the cocktails and garnish each dish with a prawn and a lemon slice. Serve the cocktails with the brown bread, if using.

WOK-FRIED KING PRAWNS IN SPICY SAUCE

SERVES 4

INGREDIENTS

- 3 TBSP VEGETABLE OR GROUNDNUT OIL
- 450 G/1 LB RAW KING PRAWNS, UNPEELED
- 2 TSP FINELY CHOPPED FRESH GINGER
- 1 TSP FINELY CHOPPED GARLIC
- 1 TBSP CHOPPED SPRING ONION
- 2 TBSP CHILLI BEAN SAUCE
- 1 TSP SHAOXING RICE WINE
- 1 TSP SUGAR
- ½ TSP LIGHT SOY SAUCE
- 1–2 TBSP CHICKEN STOCK

1 In a preheated wok or deep saucepan, heat the oil, toss in the prawns and stir-fry over a high heat for about 4 minutes. Arrange the prawns on the sides of the wok, out of the oil, then add the ginger and garlic and stir until fragrant. Add the spring onion and chilli bean sauce. Stir the prawns into the mixture.

2 Reduce the heat slightly and add the rice wine, sugar, soy sauce and stock. Cover and cook for a further minute. Serve immediately.

SCALLOPS WITH BREADCRUMBS & PARSLEY

SERVES 4

INGREDIENTS

- 20 LARGE FRESH SCALLOPS, ABOUT 4 CM/1½ INCHES THICK, REMOVED FROM THEIR SHELLS
- 200 G/7 OZ CLARIFIED BUTTER
- 85 G/3 OZ DAY-OLD FRENCH BREAD, MADE INTO FINE BREADCRUMBS
- 5 TBSP FINELY CHOPPED FRESH FLAT-LEAF PARSLEY
- SALT AND PEPPER
- LEMON WEDGES, TO SERVE (OPTIONAL)

1 Preheat the oven to its lowest temperature. Use a small knife to remove the dark vein that runs around each scallop, then rinse and pat dry. Season to taste with salt and pepper and set aside.

2 Melt half the butter in a large sauté or frying pan over a high heat. Add the breadcrumbs, reduce the heat to medium and fry, stirring, for 5–6 minutes, or until they are golden brown and crisp. Remove the breadcrumbs from the pan, drain well on kitchen paper, then keep warm in the oven. Wipe out the pan.

3 Use 2 large sauté or frying pans to cook all the scallops at once without overcrowding the pans. Melt 50 g/1¾ oz of the butter in each pan over a high heat. Reduce the heat to medium, divide the scallops between the 2 pans in single layers and fry for 2 minutes.

4 Turn the scallops over and fry for a further 2–3 minutes, or until they are golden and cooked through – cut one with a knife to check. Add extra butter to the pans if necessary.

5 Mix the breadcrumbs and parsley together, divide the scallops between 4 warmed plates and sprinkle with the breadcrumbs and parsley mixture. Serve with lemon wedges for squeezing over, if using.

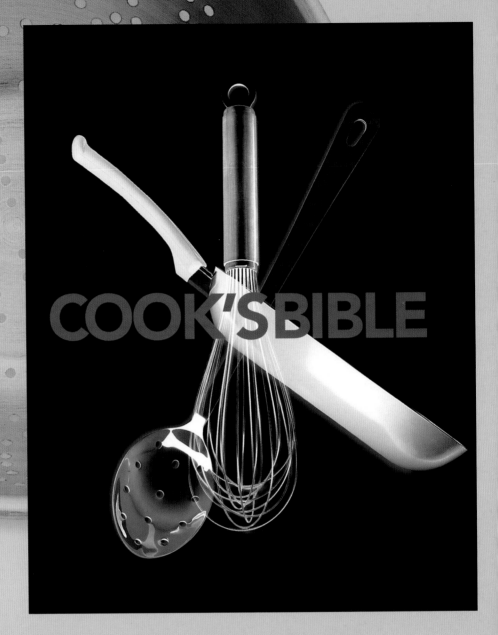

COOK'SBIBLE

ALSO AVAILABLE IN MARKS & SPENCER
ARE A WIDE RANGE OF INSPIRATIONAL
COOKBOOKS INCLUDING THE BESTSELLING
FOOD BIBLE COLLECTION

Visit your local M&S for more details;
all titles listed are subject to availability.

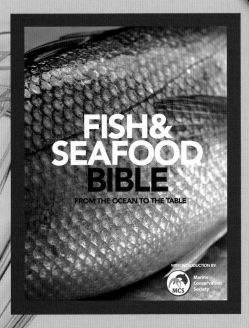

FISH&
SEAFOOD
BIBLE

FROM THE OCEAN TO THE TABLE

WITH INTRODUCTION BY:

Marine
Conservation
Society
MCS

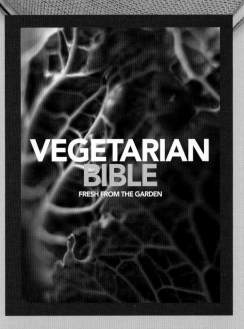

VEGETARIAN
BIBLE

FRESH FROM THE GARDEN

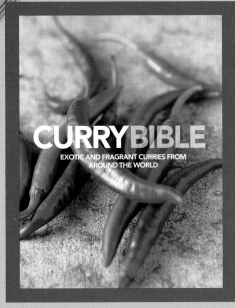

CURRY BIBLE

**EXOTIC AND FRAGRANT CURRIES FROM
AROUND THE WORLD**

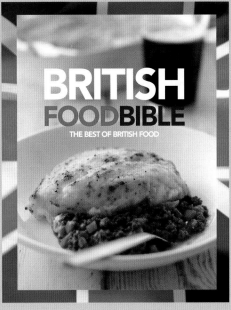

BRITISH
FOOD BIBLE

THE BEST OF BRITISH FOOD